A NOTE FROM THE SERIES EDITOR

The Inspirational range from Trigger brings you genuine stories about our authors' experiences with mental health problems.

Some of the stories in our Inspirational range will move you to tears.

Some will make you laugh. Some will make you feel angry, or surprised, or uplifted. Hopefully they will all change the way you see mental health problems.

These are stories we can all relate to and engage with. Stories of people experiencing mental health difficulties and finding their own ways to overcome them with dignity, humour, perseverance and spirit.

Love and Other Gods tells a story we don't hear quite so often; of a South Asian man trying to find himself between two worlds, suffering from mental illness along the way. Michael tells his story honestly and with courage, shedding light on his journey and all that he faced. Lyrically told, this is a book unlike any other we have published before.

This is our Inspirational range. These are our stories. We hope you enjoy them. And most of all, we hope that they will educate and inspire you. That's what this range is all about.

Lauren Callaghan,
Co-founder and Lead Consultant Psychologist at Trigger

TRIGGER™

The mental health & wellbeing publisher

www.triggerpublishing.com

The**inspirational**series™
Overcoming adversity and thriving

Love and Other Gods
ADVENTURES THROUGH PSYCHOSIS

BY MICHAEL NANGLA

We are proud to introduce The**inspirational**series™. Part of the Trigger family of innovative mental health books, The**inspirational**series™ tells the stories of the people who have battled and beaten mental health issues. For more information visit: www.triggerpublishing.com

THE AUTHOR

Born to Sikh parents in 1967, Michael is the youngest of a proudly traditional family, and is the only member to be born in England, something that has deeply defined him as he reconciles his two cultures. He grew up in Leeds before moving to Cardiff and Warwick to study philosophy. He became a journalist, covering the politics of the early noughties, before becoming a documentary producer for BBC Radio 4.

Having run away to Paris to be a writer in his early twenties, he is now realising that dream back in London, where he lives with his wife, Sevim, and their daughter, Hayal. He has all that he always yearned for underneath the all-consuming search for truth which he thought defined him. As his uncle in India once advised, knowledge isn't everything and sometimes happiness is all that matters.

First published in Great Britain 2019 by Trigger

Trigger is a trading style of Shaw Callaghan Ltd & Shaw Callaghan 23 USA, INC.

The Foundation Centre

Navigation House, 48 Millgate, Newark

Nottinghamshire NG24 4TS UK

www.triggerpublishing.com

British Library Cataloguing in Publication Data

A CIP catalogue record for this book is available upon request
from the British Library

ISBN: 978-1-78956-082-4

This book is also available in the following e-Book and Audio formats:

MOBI: 978-1-78956-085-5

EPUB: 978-1-78956-083-1

Cover design and typeset by Fusion Graphic Design Ltd

Printed and bound in Great Britain by Clays Ltd, Elcograf S.p.A

Paper from responsible sources

To my wife Sevim for inspiring me;
my daughter Hayal who brought light.
And to the memory of my parents.

To Perry,
With blessings of love &
peace.
Michael x.

Disclaimer: Some names and identifying details have been changed to protect the privacy of individuals.

PROLOGUE

'My mother had her first period on the day she was married.'

Peter, my psychiatrist, sat back a little, his hands folded together as if he was praying. 'That's interesting,' he said. 'How old was she?'

'She must have been fourteen. She never knew her real birthday. But she always remembered being around sixteen years old at the time of what she referred to as "The Separation". That was the Partition of India in 1947. She saw her Muslim elders and friends no longer feeling safe in their ancestral homes where they had lived for centuries. She experienced her community torn apart by religious bigotry and hatred. On account of their religion, Muslims were compelled to leave her village for a newly created country called Pakistan. On a scale that my mother could never comprehend, over a million people were killed in an insane slaughter. Rani, my mother, never cared much for independence.'

'How did it make you feel that your mother confided such an intimate event with you, like her menstrual cycle?' Peter continued, bringing me back to my point.

'She was irritated when I didn't know what a "monthly" was. I was only eleven when she told me. I remember feeling ashamed, especially since she was so proud of me for being clever. I thought I'd let her down.' I pictured my mother clothed in nuptial red and gold, being carried in a wedding palanquin along dusty roads far away from her village in the Punjab to a new home, anticipating meeting her tender husband, feeling afraid that she was bleeding.

Peter looked at me with an unfazed gaze, inviting me to talk freely without fear.

'And why is knowing about your mother's period significant for you?'

'She didn't go to school and never regretted it. My mother was happy. She could only tell the time by the rising and setting of the sun. Everything she knew about life was gleaned from the language and sensations of her body. She chose to reveal herself to me, so that I might better understand the origins of my own being. Telling me about her period was a way of passing onto me her knowledge, that life and death are not dissimilar. And that it was her belief that my destiny was written in a stateless existing prior to conception.'

'Did you believe her?' Peter said. 'What I mean is, do you have an idea that you existed in some way prior to being born?'

I felt tearful. My heart beat faster, the muscles in my chest tightened. 'Yes, I think so. Instead of being able to know who I am here and now, my mother conditioned me to see myself as being otherworldly. She'd given birth to nine children. Four of them died early in childhood or soon after birth. I am the youngest of five remaining siblings. My mother was in her mid-to-late forties when I was conceived. She proudly told everyone that she created my embryo by scraping together all the blood and leftovers inside her uterus.'

'It's as if she was an artisan,' Peter said.

'Yes, she was the creator of my life and fate. It wasn't just the fact that I had been born that was important for her, but also what or who I may have been before being planted in her womb.'

*

I had been seeing Peter every week for three years at his practice in Harley Street, to figure out why I was prone to having psychotic episodes. It had taken all this time for me to begin talking more candidly about the people and events that had imprinted themselves in my biography.

We were on the fifth floor of a Georgian mansion. Often, when my concentration flagged, I'd look out of the window, watching the translucent play of light and shade across the western sky.

As the session drew to a close, I felt relaxed with my sense of possessing several lives, each one with a different beginning and ending, which I was trying to disentangle in order to overcome the ceaseless malaise afflicting me. Peter was my guide in an important work: to create a unified story out of misaligned fragments, sculpting meaning out of the madness I had experienced.

*

By most accounts, I have failed in my life. I have no job. My mental ill health seems to have condemned me to a life of forced indolence. But it's my choice to reject a world that is fake. I have chosen to reconstruct my life according to my own edicts. I often despair when unearthing the past – resurrection is not for everyone. I write in the hope that it will bring credence to my life, that somehow I'll emerge from it as an integrated human being. I don't accept the common idea of letting go. I'm quite fond of the spectres that have wrecked me.

PART ONE

1

I was nineteen at the time. It was my first year in college in Cardiff, living away from home. A friend of mine called Devi told me about this Indian girl going crazy in the women's toilet of the Students' Union. Devi said that the woman was distressed and crying, 'Can anyone stop this fucking bleeding? Will someone please help?' I pictured a fragile Indian girl soaked in tears, banging her head against the tampon machine mourning a miscarriage.

I was much younger then, trying to unravel what makes us human and life what it is, the understanding of which will always elude me. Even though I hadn't seen or known her, listening to Devi, I felt an immense empathy and a sincere need to answer that young woman's call for help. I often remembered that image of the young woman as I imagined her, hurting herself, pleading with others to rescue her from her tremendous fear and pain.

From Devi's description, I recognised the woman, seeing her occasionally from afar, in and around the university. Her name was Anarkali. I wondered how she was coping. It was strange knowing about an intimate moment in her life without having any connection with her.

It was the first time that I fancied someone who was – like me – an Indian. Until this moment, I had mistakenly believed that every Asian immigrant in Britain was a relation of mine: an uncle, aunt, brother or sister. I was naturally shy and felt it would be too intrusive to approach her. I never had the courage to talk to her but, like a voyeur, observed her closely whenever she happened to pass, walking alone as if immersed in a pool of loneliness.

There were times when I was close enough to make my existence known to Anarkali, like in the club where I danced awkwardly to REM's 'Losing my Religion' desperately wanting her to notice me. She was drunk and dancing with her back pressed closely against a tall man. She was gazing in my direction. Her movement was slow and out of tempo with the song. One hand rested on the curve of her hip, while the other cradled the man's head as he kissed the nape of her neck. She wore glossy red lipstick and thick mascara highlighting a faraway look. Then she lifted her skirt to reveal her knickers with black polka dots. I noticed how dejected Anarkali seemed – she was disconnected from her surroundings, going through the motions but caught elsewhere in unhappy thoughts. For me, it was both tragic and repulsive that at the end of the night she would end up having sex with a stranger.

Perhaps I despised Anarkali then. Actually, I was jealous. I too wanted to be liberated from my own repressions. I couldn't get a hard-on without feeling thrilled and ashamed at the same time. Raw sexual energy had no place in my romantic repertoire of images. Instead, shame made me retreat into a naïve idealism. I timidly professed love for women I slept with, concealing my ignorance about who they really were in their essence. I felt frightened by the stirrings of sexuality in my body – I found it difficult to distinguish between the fine line dividing the metaphorical from what is permissible in intimate acts.

In what way did I want to devour women or be devoured by them?

*

I downed a bottle of wine feeling forlorn. Some women came up to me.

'You havin' a good time, love?' one of them said in a lilting South Wales accent.

'Why shouldn't I be? There are people dying of hunger around the world. We're having fun, aren't we?' I said.

I headed home through the litter-strewn city, stumbling, feeling heartsick. Eventually, I arrived in the square enclosed with sycamore trees where I lived. I always smiled when I saw this place because it represented freedom for me, as it was the first space I could call my own.

*

I was away from the small overcrowded red bricked terraced house where I grew up in Leeds in West Yorkshire. I had shared an attic with my mum and dad up until the day I left to come study at university. Sometimes they were kind towards each other, sometimes they bickered about petty things, like too much salt in the food or the amount of money my father gave my mother for running the home. Indeed, whose home was it anyway?

'I bore these children, I raised them,' my mother said.

'And I have worked all my life for you,' said my father.

'What work do you do? You come home drunk every night.'

'Where is your respect for me?'

'You're a loafer.'

'How dare you!'

'Don't threaten me or I'll show you.'

My mother tended to beat my father in every argument. Mostly he retreated to drink at the threat of violence. She said many things in anger about him that were untrue, but even then, her sentences contained elements of what was real. There is no doubt that there existed a deep inseparable bond between them. They had essentially grown up together, experiencing the panoply of what life gave: joy, hardship, grief... But my mother's perennial complaint in Britain as time went on was of being side-lined in important family decisions, becoming disenfranchised as her husband and children became more successful, the meat eating and alcohol drinking more copious.

*

By the time I reached my teens in the mid-1980s, I had become an idealistic bystander who rejoiced in other people's pronouncements of love, but I seldom met anyone who was really happy. It often came as a genuine surprise and I took it as a personal affront when friends ended relationships. Their lives appeared to be a lie, set against the pitiful recriminations over who betrayed the other. I wanted to believe that love really existed, but the ease with which people manufactured fall-outs showed me that it was a sham.

That night after the club, I crawled into bed alone unable to take my mind off Anarkali. I felt so lonely and I thought it was because I didn't have her beside me. I wanted so much to be lying next to her, holding her hand. I turned over and vomited on the carpet. I was in love with her. Despite her bawdy display, I wanted to hold her and be cared for by her. There was part of me that also wanted to be promiscuous like her. For me, she epitomised someone who was archetypally both wise and a harlot at the same time, like a Madonna and Magdalene. I felt she would initiate me into the mysteries of life, obliterating mundane conformity.

For years, Anarkali remained a beautiful unattainable fantasy. I never did approach her and I left the city having graduated with my first degree without ever introducing myself. I felt uneasy about returning to my family because I thought I hadn't acquired or learnt anything valuable, so I decided – to my father's consternation – to extend my studies. I went to Warwick University where I absorbed myself in Continental Philosophy.

2

I am living amongst the stars of the cosmos, cycling in the land surrounding Warwick, looking for signs of God projecting himself in the countryside from out of the wild fog of his untamed mind. I sense his nearness in the footprints left by cattle and sheep on the earth, in blades of grass touched by the breeze and the night song of running streams. Every evening, I buy a can of Sapporo from Oddbins, where Susan serves me. She has her hair in a bob in the style of Louise Brooks. I can feel the gentleness of her hands as she gives me the change. I desire to kiss her because of the way she welcomes me, the warmth of her eyes, the fullness of her smile. I cycle with my can of beer in one hand through fields of twilit yellow rape singing songs to myself. I have become a bright-eyed Hegelian and have never found myself so interesting. I have invited myself to celebrate life.

It's been a long time since I've been awake to the beauty of life. I feel closer than ever to my mother who was too depressed to pick me up in my first few months. All my brothers and sisters had been born with the help of Nanda, the midwife in my parents' village in India. I, on the other hand, arrived in the alien clinicality of a hospital, on a spring day in the north of England with male doctors instructing my mother in a language she didn't understand. Did they mime what they expected her to do? Did they touch her in ways that made her feel uncomfortable? I suppose she drew on Nanda's knowledge of breathing out powerfully. I was put in a glass cradle, then taken away from my mother who must have felt helpless. My life wasn't in her hands at that moment and she couldn't bond with me. I was an ugly child: 'Like a monkey all covered in hair,' she said. In my later years, she grew to show a fidelity, which I cherished though deep down felt unworthy of.

I read Hegel religiously every night in my basement digs. I could see the legs of people passing overhead from a light well that opened up onto the pavement. Under the spotlight of my desk lamp, I wrestled with sentences that barely made sense, trying to understand what it meant when he said that the work of life could begin only after death had been preserved. While I did daily things like walk through the modernist university campus, shop for cheap food in the supermarket near where I lived or just listen to music, I began having a sense of the meaning of the Passion of Christ and his redemption as the Son of Man. The terrifying torture that Christ underwent dawned in my imagination – the sorrow a human being has to endure for the truth that justice, freedom, and love are the only real values embedded within human life. I'd sit listening to the ticking of the second hand on the timepiece while picturing a lonely man hanging on a cross covered in a cloud of incomprehension.

Reading Hegel liberated me from the habit of living with duality: the alienation between the earthly and the divine, male and female, Indian and British, child and adult... Hegel called his time the end of history, as he alone had realised that ultimately consciousness and matter, you and I, are identical but nonetheless still distinct. This insight brought about an awakening for me characterised by the bliss I felt. Everything was part of me and I a part of it. If I had been an angel, I would have cast aside my wings and not been afraid to walk amongst people.

I could no longer be a spectator of other people's wanting for love but needed to experience it in my own flesh. I felt unafraid of life and myself for the first time. I wanted to embrace my mother and my lovers, completely acting in a way that was true to me.

My world became a theatre in which women played the main roles. I would watch them, fascinated to see how their smallest gestures expressed the most profound things. I remember thinking that the women who looked at themselves in their compact mirrors to put makeup on were not vain as others thought, but that they were checking themselves to see if they were real or not.

It was on one of these heightened days that I saw Astrid in the library between shelves of books. She wore a black skirt with a white lace hem.

Curiosity about my feelings for Astrid made me follow her out of the building into the falling rain. I walked towards her awkwardly. 'Excuse me. I'm sorry. You don't know me. But I would like to get to know you better, because you intrigue me.'

She blushed and hesitated. 'Why is that?'

'I'm finding it difficult to describe. I think it's the way you hold your books close to your chest.'

'There's not much reason in liking that.'

'No, that's true. But I am drawn to you. Will you join me for a coffee?'

'Thank you for asking. But I'm really busy.'

'Where do you live?'

'In Leamington.'

'Look, I've never done this before. My name is Michael Nangla and this is my telephone number. Maybe when you have time?'

I scribbled my number. She took the piece of paper and walked away.

I thought about her every day.

She eventually called after two weeks. 'Hi, do you remember me?'

'Yes, of course I do. My mother is the only other woman who calls me.'

Astrid laughed. 'I don't know if that's a compliment or something I should be worried about. I wondered if you were still on for meeting. My friends are doing other things. I have some free time.'

'Would you like to go to this bistro called Harry's Bar? It's near where I live, just off the Caledonian Road.'

'That'll be nice. When?'

'When's good for you?'

'How about tonight?' I asked hopefully.

'I'm afraid I can't tonight. How about tomorrow evening?'

'Wonderful. Let's meet tomorrow. Is half seven good for you?'

'Yes, for certain. I'll meet you there.'

Harry's Bar was a dimly lit place, set in the lower ground floor of an old decaying building. Walking into it felt like entering a Parisian joint on the Left Bank in the 1960s. We were led by a waiter dressed in a black waistcoat, white shirt, black trousers, and patent leather shoes to one of the tables covered in red-and-white chequered cloths, with candles stuck in old wine bottles. Astrid and I sat opposite each other.

'I like it,' she said, looking around at the other staff, while listening to 'A Love Supreme' by John Coltrane that was being played. 'The waiters here are very urbane. It's rare to find people who really care about their work.'

I was struck by her insight. I looked at her porcelain complexion tinged with rose pink, disbelieving that we were actually together.

'What do you study?' I asked.

'Art History,' she said.

'That's interesting.'

'I don't know if I'm any good, but it's a wonderful subject.'

'What's your favourite period?'

'I love the Renaissance. They captured something magical in their everyday lives like Jesus being baptised in the River Tiber

– an event, which happened in Palestine, an imaginary place no one had visited, set in the reality of fifteenth-century Rome. But my favourite period is the Impressionists. I love Monet and can spend hours looking at his gardens.'

'What about Picasso and the Expressionists?'

She smiled playfully. 'Yes, Picasso is wonderful. But the Expressionists are far too dark and psychological for me'.

Astrid was eloquent but modest. We drank many glasses of wine, she enjoyed Rioja and I opted for Cotes Du Rhone. We shared a platter of cheeses with grapes. I relaxed, becoming more enamoured with her as the evening wound on. Towards midnight, the staff at Harry's were getting ready to close.

'Would you like to come back to my place for a drink?' I asked.

'I think I've drunk far too much. But tea would be nice,' she said.

It was the first time I allowed myself to experience lust as a passion without covering it with the patina of a sublime idea. I wanted so much to uncover Astrid, to see her for who she was. We walked close to each other the short distance to my house. I made her tea, coffee for myself. We went to my bedroom. I put on my cassette player as background music. We talked about the weather. She sensed my nervousness and now that it was late, she volunteered to leave.

'Do you want to stay?' I asked.

'I'm not sure,' she said. 'It's been a lovely evening. I don't want to spoil it.'

I felt offended. I wasn't sure what she meant. Was she assuming I wanted to sleep with her? And besides, she wasn't answering my question.

'Why don't we throw a coin? Heads, you stay. Tails, you leave,' I said.

We sat on the floor flipping a coin. It went to the best of three. It became more obvious that both of us wanted to spend the night together, regardless of the outcome of a coin. I gave her my vintage long French cotton shirt to sleep in. We got into bed. There was a moment she looked questioningly into my eyes; then she touched my lips with her fingers, as if mapping out a target and kissed me.

'May I touch your breast?'

She smiled. 'Yes, please.'

When I kissed her breasts, it was if it had been many lifetimes since I had laid my head on a woman's body. Everything about Astrid aroused me: her hair, her eyes, the undulating terrain of her body, the scent of ylang-ylang, and her sibilant speech. I was closing a door on my childhood. I wanted to remain with her for the rest of my life.

We lay together quietly watching the flickering shadows on the wall cast by gentle candlelight. She held my hand, her face turned away from me. She quivered against my touch. Her pale body contrasted with my brown skin. There was the occasional sound of someone passing overhead on an otherwise quiet street. My heart was full and my head empty. I curled up like a vulnerable child cupping his knees against his chest needing protection from the world listening to her rhythmic breathing and the alarm clock on the dresser lulling time. I fell asleep knowing I felt safe beside her.

3

My mother had been pregnant with her ninth child. She was expecting to go into labour very soon. That year the monsoon was particularly fierce. The warm rains lashed down on the verdant terrain watering the lush paddy fields and tall sugar cane. My father who had been a tailor in India had made the acquaintance of a former British Army officer who had agreed to sponsor his voyage to England in the 1960s. The official papers arrived but for some unknown reason it was decided that he should leave straightaway. My mother always recalled it as an act of great sacrifice. It was on the night of a savage storm when she was very sick that my father came to her room to say goodbye. Seeing her looking weak and ill, he was overcome with self-doubt not knowing what to do. My mother garnered the little strength she had and told him, 'You must leave. We've our family to think of. Don't worry about us since everything is in God's hands. You mustn't let go of this chance. I and the children will wait for you.' He left that night giving her one rupee.

*

A boy was born in the early hours of a Wednesday morning, so my mother named him 'Budh,' after the Punjabi word for that day of the week. Both mother and child were poorly and he couldn't latch on sufficiently to get his nutrition. My father never saw his son who died three weeks after being born. Although she never forgot the four other children who died early, my mother had ascribed their early passing away to the numinous play of nature and fate. But she always bore a special attachment to Budh. In my father's absence, she'd felt even more personally responsible for the child's survival and tried with all her being to rescue him. Inevitably, she carried a sense of failing him throughout her life. My mother always grieved with the memory of the boy's funeral. He couldn't be cremated because according to Vedic tradition he was too young. In the end, she gave my brother's body wrapped in a white cotton shroud to the caretaker of a Muslim Sufi shrine on the fringes of the village. It was a great comfort to her that her son was buried on holy ground.

My mother always managed to salvage something positive from the most dire of situations. Many years later, she claimed that the boy whose life she'd failed to save had miraculously reappeared again and that her deepest prayers had been answered. She thought I was his reincarnation. From a young age, I felt covered by the shadow of my brother who had died far away and in some ways guilty for perhaps having been the cause of his death, since a space had to be made for me to enter the world.

4

Astrid woke up early. She put on her clothes.

'It was really lovely, Michael. But I have to go. My boyfriend might be home and wondering where I am.'

I was bewildered. It was the first time she had mentioned anything about a boyfriend. I kept my rising feelings of hurt at bay.

'Will you come back to me?' I asked.

'Yes. I'll explain later.'

I don't know that I understood, but her answer at least gave me some hope.

She came round to my place after college. We sat at the kitchen table on which there was a vase of wild flowers that I had gathered from one of my walks to the hedgerows nearby. Late afternoon sparkles of sunshine streamed through the dirty window lighting up the smoky room. The ashtray was full. There were long silences. She sat smiling in my direction stirring up emotions that made me feel a little drunk. Then in a thoughtful and measured tone, she said, 'I didn't intend to hide anything from you. I do have a boyfriend, but our relationship is in limbo. Although we live together, he is sleeping with another woman. I've become a nuisance for him.'

'Do you still care for him?' I said, hoping to find out whether she loved me.

'I'm confused. I don't want to deny that I still love him. We've been together so many years; I don't want to lose that. But last night I felt loved again.'

Astrid was on the rebound. She had wanted to sleep with me in order to numb the pain of her boyfriend's infidelity. I was miserable. What I thought had been seduction had actually been planned by her all along.

For a long time in their relationship, Astrid had an intimation that her boyfriend was seeing another woman.

'He used to go out every night saying he was meeting up with friends. But I sensed he was lying,' she said.

'How can you be so sure?' I said.

'One night when he was out, I went through his dressing table. I found his box of condoms was missing. When he came back, he smelt of someone else's body. All of our friends were covering up for him. I couldn't bear it any longer. Instead of talking to him, I went to them to know what was going on. I felt completely humiliated. It all happened a few months back. Now I just feel really sad. Sometimes I feel like quitting my studies and travelling somewhere far away to forget him. Do you understand?'

'I think so,' I replied. 'What your boyfriend did isn't a reflection of your worth as a human being. The Buddha said attachment is the cause of suffering. He could easily have said that it is rejection. I wish I could be of more help.'

'But you've already helped me.'

Her boyfriend's deceit had left Astrid in a state of bereavement. She often cried but then brushed aside her emotions as sentimental nonsense. I could tell that she valued me by the way she touched me and the care with which she once chose a polo neck for me. Nevertheless, I became an object for her, a means to an end. My part in Astrid's story was to fill the lack of esteem she felt. Her body needed to erase and be cleansed of her boyfriend's last caresses. I, on the other hand, wanted to serve her. I didn't mind bearing the pain she caused me. I guessed I would be hurt by her. In hindsight, my being in a relationship with Astrid was an act of self-harming.

I was beginning to realise that my understanding of emotional pain was vague. I was often distant from people who were suffering; their painful emotions left me perplexed and unable to meet or understand them. Perhaps this lack of empathy had been conditioned by those early months when my mother couldn't bear to look at me and I never felt her warmth. My way of defending myself had always been to escape into theoretical abstractions about life and human nature. I couldn't connect with the primal pain I felt at the core of who I was, but I did know that it had something to do with encountering other people in their strange, often overwhelming otherness. Until now, I had been afraid of others who appeared to exist like mirages – I found their presence in my world oppressive. I had enjoyed being alone, but it was an unhappy existence. Being with Astrid, I felt an urgent need to experience real life. I was driven to dismantle the barriers I had built separating myself from the things around me. I revered Astrid so much that I felt a need to heal the separation between myself and others; I needed to sanctify once again the space between I and Thou. I wanted to feel the power of my empathy. How much pain could I endure before finally walking away? How much self-abasement could there be to free me from my attachment to my mother, allowing me to forgive how she refused me as a baby?

Over the next several months, Astrid and I took to spending hours in a noisy workers' café with plastic school chairs and desks for tables in Leamington Spa. We spoke to each other about things that mattered most to us. She recalled what attracted her to her boyfriend while I tried uselessly expressing what I meant by the sublime from my reading of Romantic poetry. I felt happy in her presence. With this also came a retrospective regret about how I must have casually hurt women in the past who had wanted to befriend me and become lovers of mine, except I had been too afraid. Before Astrid, I didn't feel I could ever commit myself to any one person. Being with her changed the way I felt about sex. For the first time, sex did not depress me because I was able to present myself to her – in the sense of being in the here and now, letting myself be vulnerable. I longed to give Astrid pleasure, even though the ephemerality of it still continued to bother me.

*

One night after orgasm I sat on the window ledge, feeling a warm breeze brushing my naked body. The yew trees in front were swaying, the air was pungent with summer's smell and the sky was a field of lavender. I looked at my shadow strewn across the lawn below. I felt at peace with the world. At high moments like this, it was my habit to sing or recite poetry to give expression to the body of emotions that danced inside me. Some lines from Shakespeare's *Othello* came to my mind. This impulse didn't just arise from identifying myself as a black man with a trophy white woman – I felt comfort in reciting English poetry because it gave me a sense of esteem and belonging, which I ordinarily wasn't permitted to feel in white British society. The passionate wisdom of Shakespeare's words were a compass enabling me to locate myself in England and connect with my inner soul. I whispered:

... If it were now to die,
'Twere now to be most happy; for I fear
My soul hath her content so absolute
That not another comfort like to this
Succeeds in in unknown fate [1]

Astrid lay covered in a white Egyptian cotton sheet. Sleepily, she said, 'What was that?'

'It's a beautiful evening,' I replied.

*

My shadow was seducing me to jump, because I felt that to die young was a blessing – to extinguish oneself at the apex of love without ever experiencing its misery. Instead, I sat motionless; the trees, the stars, and the lights in opposite apartments looked back at me. When we woke up in the morning, there was blood on the sheets. She'd had her period.

'Look,' I said. 'You've menstruated in the shape of a heart.' It was an erotic moment since symbolically the crimson heart bled onto the white sheet, epitomised the intensity of my feeling and lovemaking. I felt that I had kissed her soul. Astrid was speechless.

I sensed she would feel compelled to leave me.

It was the end of term. Astrid's boyfriend finally left for good. The spluttering flame of love that still burnt inside her was finally put out. She felt wretched. The love she thought had been immeasurable, had been weighed, dissected, and tossed aside. Her fantasy of being reconciled with him had been dispelled.

Astrid and I cycled out to the fields near our university. I looked at her hair and Indian-printed skirt billowing in the wind as we pedalled. Mist floated wispily above the land. It was dusk, swallows wheeled and circled in a rose madder sky. I was sad for her but also excited that at last she might return my longing.

We stopped and sat on a bench gazing into the distance.

'I'm sorry for you,' I said.

'He left without saying goodbye. I don't think I'll ever see him again,' she replied. 'I don't think he ever loved me.'

She rested her head on my shoulder. I felt content. Even though I was beside her, I was alone. I was dreaming of living a peaceful, perpetually young life with her, all the time painfully aware of its impossibility. It was too soon for Astrid. She was mourning the loss of her idealism. She knew I loved her but had chosen to ignore – or worse neglect – the scent of my affection. Not far away, in the close distance, there were two horses tethered to a wooden baton stuck in the damp ground. They looked totally harmonious making a beautiful figure in the dissolving light. Time was passing – the quiet intensifying.

'Do you still want to go the party?' I asked.

She nodded.

We got on our bicycles and headed home.

That night we went to a house packed with young people standing, sitting or dancing to trance music being played on turntables in a smoky, spacious red–carpeted living room. There were people smoking marijuana and resin, others absorbed in loud conversations, drinking beer or red wine. The room was intoxicated with the excitement of dreamers and fatalists who had barely crossed the threshold of adolescence, saying goodbye to college friends to pursue new, as yet unwritten, lives.

We felt and looked beautiful.

How many of us would turn ugly in the duel with the world and ourselves?

Astrid and I sat on the floor, in a corner holding hands. I treasured that feeling. A friend of mine called Anthony, from philosophy class caught my attention. I went over to him and we began talking about Andrei Tarkovsky's film *Stalker*, which we had both seen recently. I was so engrossed that when I looked back, I saw that Astrid was gone.

I began looking for her through the crowd, beginning to feel sick in my stomach. After what seemed a long time, I stood feeling tired and confused outside a room with a closed door. There was nowhere else to go. My heart was breaking. I opened the door and saw Astrid there with a tall man. He had her pinned against a wall, her arms high above her head as if she was surrendering in battle. Their faces were locked together. She saw me but continued kissing him. I shut the door on the scene. I stood there waiting for her a little like a dog tied up by its owner outside of a shop. Astrid came out. I couldn't look at her. My head was bowed.

'Do you mind if I stay with him tonight?' she said.

'Why are you asking for my permission? Do what you like,' I said.

She stroked the side of my face nonchalantly at arm's length. I felt her pity and bitterness at having to attend to me. Her eyes were distant and opaque.

'I'm coming with you,' she said, leading the way.

I followed her obediently.

We walked, unable to talk, through the streets of Leamington before sunrise, past houses with white facades, and gardens beginning to wake in summer blush to the rising sound of birds. In the distance was a church with a tall spire, dwarfed by giant cooling towers that spewed mountains of smoke into a purple sky. There was a tramp in the doorway of a betting shop touting for change. I felt helpless against the swathe of emotions and humiliation, mixed with an awkward feeling of triumph at being a victim. I could find no ethical injunction requiring Astrid to behave loyally towards me but being a victim in this case kept open the possibility of entrapping her in a relationship with me. I walked unsteadily, still a little drunk. Strange as it may seem, I valued unconditionally Astrid's freedom to be and do as she pleased. I needed her to want me for who I was – not on the basis of some preconditioned imperative. Love has no conditions. Freedom, I believe is the soul of love.

We staggered along the meandering streets. Then Astrid broke the silence. 'I'm not going to make love with you,' she said.

I stopped in the middle of the pavement.

'I don't want you to,' I said.

She sensed my resentment. I looked for signs of remorse or guilt from her, but there were none. She looked questioningly at me, as if trying to work me out.

'You're the one who said that freedom and love are the same thing. What happened to those ideals?'

'I thought we were together.'

'We're not, Michael. I'm a woman trying to forget her past. That man in there was the only one I fancied while going out with Matthew. I wasn't being unfaithful to you, but to my old boyfriend. Do you understand?'

I didn't understand, but I knew we were both hurting.

We arrived at Astrid's house. We went up the stairs to her bedroom. She lit some incense. We sat on her mattress on the floor. Then Astrid put her arms around me and began weeping. The wetness on my neck felt uncomfortable; I wanted to pull away, but stayed holding her, unable to let go. Sunlight began entering the room. We lay down together in each other's limp embrace, both tired and broken.

A calm period followed. Astrid took refuge in the love that I gave her. We were together nearly every night for the next few weeks. We sometimes watched the games of the 1990 Football World Cup on TV. We were happy hiding away from our families. Being found out would have meant ostracisation. Her parents would have thought that no white man would ever touch her again whereas for me there was the shame because unsanctioned sex was strictly prohibited.

Mornings were especially pleasurable. She often breakfasted on muesli and yoghurt but I made her splendid French toast, sweetened with freshly squeezed orange juice and dusted with ground cinnamon. For my birthday, she brought me a bundle of fresh herbs and exotic spices. That evening, I used the natural gifts to cook potatoes and cauliflower. When we ate, it was like a communion. I was moved. I was consenting for her to consume my spirit-body with each mouthful of the food I had lovingly prepared. From now on, I was willing to transgress the limitations placed on me by my conservative Indian upbringing. It was unacceptable to my family and community that I should have relations with any woman that was not first vetted by them.

Being with a white woman who neither belonged to nor could understand our culture was a shameful taboo. My mother was always more accepting of the outside world. She wished me to live according to my inner principles and was seen by my insular community as a dangerous influence. Bigoted pragmatists conveniently demonised her as being a little mad. Despite the fear, being with Astrid compelled me to cast myself mentally adrift from my father and culture into an uncharted forbidding sea.

*

One day, in the summer before leaving to go to Warwick University, before even meeting Astrid, I sat with my father in our restaurant. He was wearing his customary tweed jacket, drinking a pint of Tetley's bitter. He had no idea how anxious I was about leaving. I was struggling to tell him that I loved him and thank him for allowing me to go my way. I knew he wished for nothing more than to see me happy and to leave me an inheritance after he died. He saw me as his capital, his prize investment. I wanted to ease his burden by saying, 'Dad, I don't want any part of your money.' It was then that, on an impulse, I told him the story of the Prodigal Son. He listened intently to Jesus's parable.

'There was a son who left his father. He took with him part of his father's estate and spent it all on a debauched life. He fell on difficult times. There was a famine in the country and the boy had to work looking after pigs. When he began to envy the food he gave the animals, he regretted his disobedience. He decided to return to his father and beg his forgiveness. While on his way back, the young son decided to tell his father, "I have sinned against heaven, and against you. I am no longer worthy to be called your son. Treat me as one of your servants." The father saw his son coming in the distance; he was filled with compassion and he ran to the boy kissing him with joy at his safe return. He ordered his servants to kill the fatted calf. But the other son who had been working hard in the fields was angry. He complained to his father, saying, "Look! All these years I've been slaving for you and never disobeyed your command. You never even gave me a young goat so I could celebrate with my friends. But when this son of yours who has squandered your property with prostitutes comes home, you kill the fatted calf for him!"

The father replied, "My son, everything I have is yours. But we had to celebrate and be glad, because this brother of yours was dead and is alive again. He was lost and is found."'

I don't exactly know why I told my father this story. I guessed I too would soon reject him and test his caring for me. I felt indebted to him and my brothers for providing for me. All of them had a hand in raising me, and now I was leaving them. My sympathies lay both with the Prodigal Son and his brother. My father who was aware of the jealousies of my older siblings smiled and teased me. 'I would never welcome you back, let alone kill the fatted calf,' he said.

Before going to college, some of my brothers had begun disowning me. 'You're not going to get any share of our family inheritance,' one of them said. I was too naïve and afraid to argue back. 'You've done nothing to earn it. We've worked with our dad all our lives. What have you done to deserve an equal share of what is ours, when you've contributed nothing?' He had convinced me. It was true that being the youngest I had done nothing, whereas they'd all left school early and worked hard in mills and foundries, pooling all their resources with my father's and building up a small empire of businesses.

My father had arrived in Britain with only a few pounds. He could neither read nor write in any language. He found work as a woollen spinner in a factory owned by Courtaulds. He worked mostly night shifts because they paid better. After a few years, he had saved enough money to send for his family to come here. My brothers and sister were either in or near their teens, and soon they were all working very hard. From these modest difficult beginnings, my family bought a corner shop, then a restaurant and after two decades other people saw us as being well-off. I was born a year before the Summer of Love into a tightly-knit family that was on the move and changing with the times. There are photos of my brothers looking very handsome dressed in neatly-ironed shirts with broad collars, ties and flares; my sister looked like a film star in her brightly coloured sack dresses with swirling psychedelic patterns, her hair tied up in a mini beehive.

I was my mother and father's favourite. Being the youngest, I received a lot of love. My parents believed that clever people are also virtuous. They saw both these qualities in me, because I was bilingual. A lot of times from the age of four onwards, I would act as a translator for them like at the doctor's surgery or in shops. It was strange for me as a young boy that my parents respected me. Later in life, some of my brothers who naturally wanted to be more independent became angry at the special love that I alone seemed to receive. I was going away to experience a life they'd never had, one of learning and opportunity and – in their minds – sexual freedom. My father was unable to protect me from their hurtful remarks. He chose to maintain a diplomatic silence, which I thought was weakness on his part and a tacit agreement with the fact that I had chosen to study away from home and so had rejected them.

5

The height of summer faded in a final effervescence of colour. The farms around Leamington had been harvested. Bales of bronze hay covered the fields. The time was approaching when Astrid and I would leave each other and go our separate ways. I had very little money left and was stealing books from the university bookshop.

'Why are you risking getting caught? You might not even get your degree,' Astrid said.

'I'm doing nothing wrong. Everyone has a right to a free education. Why should I pay for books I can't afford? Everyone is entitled to the acquisition of knowledge for which lack of money shouldn't be an obstacle.'

One of my prized steals was JW Goethe's sensational autobiographical novel written in 1774 called *The Sorrows of Young Werther*. I sat down one evening to read it and was unable to move until I had finished it at sunrise. I had been completely mesmerised by the tragic story of Werther, who relinquishes his reason and life preferring instead to pursue the laws of his passionate nature.

Werther fell in love with a caring woman called Charlotte, who filled him with a happiness that comes from being understood.

He idolised her every gesture. They became close friends even though she was engaged to another man called Albert, who she marries. Werther continued to see Charlotte nearly every day in the presence of her husband who accepted their platonic friendship but began to be irritated, maybe even jealous of the attention his wife was receiving. Albert stood in Werther's way. Charlotte sensed the torment Werther was enduring and knew he was deceiving himself and willing his own suicide. Werther felt trapped inside a triangle, which he thought could only end with one of them dying. One night at Christmas, unable to control himself any longer, he tried forcing a kiss from Lotte who shunned him; confused between love and anger, she cried, 'This is the last time Werther! You will never see me again!'

Werther decided to kill himself. He wrote to Albert asking to borrow a pair of pistols on the pretext that he had to go on a journey. Lotte, who was full of terrible foreboding, sent Werther the hunting pistols. Werther was exuberant on receiving the guns from the servant; for him it was a sign of Lotte's passion for him and that only he could resolve her dilemma. At midnight, Werther shot himself in the head, but it took several hours for him to die with Lotte and Albert at his bedside witnessing his excruciating pain. Only the sexton and his son (friends of Werther) were present to see that he was buried, beneath a linden tree. Goethe became sick while writing this great work. Reflecting on the tragic circumstances of Werther's dying, Goethe observed in the last line that no priest was there at the funeral.

I admired Werther for his authenticity. I thought I understood why countless impressionable young men of the time wanted to imitate and pay homage to Goethe's tragic antihero. But Astrid, who was disturbed by my fascination, may have been right to have seen him as an obsessive deluded egomaniac.

One night, Astrid and I argued. I felt incredibly sad at the prospect of being alone and was begging her to stay with me. We both knew I was asking her to remain with me forever. 'I love you, Michael, as a friend. But I'm not in love with you,' she said.

'What's wrong with me? Why can't I make you happy?' I said.

'It's not you. I just can't ever commit myself.'

'All I want is for you to acknowledge me,' I said.

'This can't work out,' she replied, expressing despair and contempt. I wrung my hands together, pleading. She turned around and said disdainfully, 'Michael, you're not Werther.'

I understood then how angry I had been with her, without ever managing to express it in words. But the resentment was there all along, concealed in the despairing exchanges and our lovemaking. The only way I could break her was by killing myself.

I was too ashamed to consider returning to the culture that I felt forced to disown. I found myself alienated in the life I had chosen to adopt. My soul retreated into my bones like the sea ebbing back after high tide. There was a feeling of emptiness, a void in my being. It felt as if my living in the world had been a journey that had now ended. The initial rapture that had propelled me into meeting Astrid had dissolved. My original sense of being incomplete was satisfied by discovering that all along, darkness is concealed in the myriad light and light in the manifold darkness. Now there was only the desolation to endure.

Our time at university had come to an end. Astrid's parents collected her boxes of books and suitcases and took them back to Salisbury where they lived. She had decided to travel by train. That day, she came to my house to say goodbye. We made small talk, avoiding anything emotional. I observed her controlled smiles with sadness and bitterness combined. 'Have you any grass you can give me?' she said.

'You don't smoke. What do you need it for?'

'I'm going to a party tonight in Salisbury. It's for a friend.'

I went upstairs to Chris's room. He was a housemate who dealt a little in drugs to fund his education. I gave him some money and bought a quarter wrapped in transparent clingfilm. I came back and gave it to Astrid, who was sat at my desk reading a stanza of a poem I had been in the middle of writing:

Through the night wept my death
And from the fragrant dampness of sunsetting
Timeless your eyes like sarcophagi ground my flesh
Love pressed petalled lips to ears
Nothing arose
Breath a faithless thorn clawed in the air
And fell as blossom on ashen earth.

'It's beautiful,' she said. 'What's it about?'
'I don't know,' I said.
'It seems so sad. I wish I could've made you happy. I want to stay longer, but I have to go now.'
'Okay. Let me come with you to the station.'

We rushed downhill to the station and found the train heading for Salisbury. Astrid boarded a carriage, anxious to be on her way. I was trying to say something, but she couldn't hear me. Her train began moving, so I began scribbling in the dirt on the window 'Love–' but the carriage pulled away before I could add 'me'. We never saw each other again.

My affair with Astrid was over. I returned home having lost my belief in western values.

*

There was no one to confide in so no one knew about Astrid. I'd sneak out of the house wearing my second-hand blue duffel coat, buy a packet of Silk Cut cigarettes, then walk into the solitary woods behind my house. I would sing aloud sad Indian film songs from the 1970s while walking beneath an arched canopy of trees. It was a cathartic way of expressing my sadness at separating from Astrid.

My mother felt my absence even when I was with her. She sat cross-legged on the floor ironing clothes. I'm lying on the bed in our attic bedroom, daydreaming. She looked at me searchingly. 'Michael, you've lost your lightness. You look really sad. I can see you're going through something painful. You can share with me and I'll always be here for you,' she said.

My father was delighted that I'd returned to the fold. He watched me proudly as I waited on tables in our restaurant. I enjoyed talking to the customers who were mostly students or locals treating their close friends and family. We used to eat our own supper after midnight while the last tables were still absorbed in intimate conversation. Sometimes, I thought my father's expressions showed he was uncomfortable with pushing me towards having an arranged marriage. Nonetheless, he believed marrying me off would save me from the dehumanising envy of my siblings. One night he told me, 'Michael, you needn't worry. Your share of the inheritance will come from the work that your mother and I have done. Consider it as a present of our love.'

'I don't want your money. I am happy the way I am. I will find a job like everyone else,' I said.

'You're an idealist. You think you're a communist but are too young to understand the value of material things. It's what I love about you,' he said.

'I don't want wealth since it ultimately corrupts. I don't want to exploit my brothers by stealing their money.'

'There is nothing wrong in putting to good the gift of wealth. If you'd had nothing like when I was a child, then you'd understand what I mean,' he said.

I felt tearful. It was disrespectful of my brothers to be bothering him about who will get the pickings at his funeral. I felt sorry for him – he thought he had left behind the legacy of generational feuds in the Punjab, only to see them reinstated amongst his own sons in Britain.

I wanted so much to please him. Why couldn't I, like countless other Indians, be content with having an arranged marriage? Why did doing my duty feel such an anathema to me? I was depressed because I knew that whoever came into my extended household would be exposed to bitter family arguments. I already felt a little bullied, and I could not protect myself, let alone any other person. Also, my mother was not ready to let me go. She was still unprepared to share me with another woman. She needed to be sure that the woman she entrusted me to would possess intelligence, compassion, and courage – these were the kind of virtues she believed made a human being truly beautiful and were needed for her son to be loved, nurtured, and preserved.

Early one evening that summer, sitting at our restaurant with the red velvet flock wallpaper, before any customers had arrived, I decided to open up to my father.

'Father,' I said, 'I believe in Guru Nanak. I cannot follow him and at the same time accept a caste system that degrades human beings. He wanted caste to be eradicated. It has to stop somewhere, why not now?' I sensed my voice getting louder and checked my emotions. 'We are all children born from the light of the One Creator. I want to enshrine the Sikh ideals of equality, love and freedom in my own life.'

'That's very beautiful. But the world is riddled with caste,' he said.

'How can I accept thousands of years of wickedness where Hindu priests have denigrated and belittled people into low ranks. Some castes were deemed less than animals – people were made to sweep away their own footprints left on the ground and make sure their shadow didn't cross any other person. Outcastes were allowed only to drink rainwater left where cattle and other animals had trodden. I don't want to be part of this.'

'It was inhuman, I know. But things have changed since then. Even those who belong to lower castes are proud of their status, and we accept that we are all part of humankind. But what are you trying to tell me?' he asked.

'I don't want an arranged marriage,' I said.

'It is a natural law that your mother and father are like God,' he said. 'You have a duty to honour us and do what we think is right for you. Our reputation depends on your marrying. Marriage will give you a place in this world. You will have your own family and our responsibilities will be eased; your mother and I will be free to concentrate on our old age.'

'I cannot be true to myself and carry out my traditional duty. It makes me unhappy that I should marry into our caste.'

'Are you ashamed of being a water carrier?'

'No,' I said. 'How can those who gave water to the thirsty ever be shameful. I'm willing to sacrifice myself for you. I'm willing to marry whoever you want, even though I don't agree with it. I will see someone and try with all my heart to say "yes". But if I refuse her, I don't want to be introduced to anyone else.'

My father's eyes were shining. We had an intimate way of communicating, often persuading each other with our convictions. We spoke in an earthy poetic Punjabi. What I have written here is an inadequate imitation, lacking the emotional juice of our exchanges. Even his gestures were fashioned in the language of the Punjab. The more I think and dream in English, the greater the distance I feel between him and me becomes. He was an uncompromising patriarch, especially when it came to my brothers. Often he was kind, but at times quite savage when criticising or punishing them when he was disobeyed. He heard what I was saying even though he was sceptical at first. I saw from his expression that he was moved by my dilemma. 'How do I know you won't decline without giving it any serious thought?' he said.

'Trust me!' I said. 'How would you feel if someone rejected your daughter? I won't refuse anyone lightly. Every woman is unique and special to her parents. I'll agree to marry who you want me to.' I didn't want my father to be worried about me any longer.

He smiled. We had found common ground. He was prepared

to loosen his control over my destiny trusting that he had my word that I would get married.

It became known on the grapevine that I had agreed to settle down. A few weeks later, a distant aunt came back with a proposal of marriage to an eighteen-year-old woman called Kirat Kaur. My family and I travelled to Coventry in two cars to meet her family on a bright cold day when leaves were beginning to turn into browns, amber, and gold. When we arrived, we were greeted with tea and samosas. Kirat's family were kind and loving people. Our fathers connected as old companions from the motherland. They talked excitedly about who they knew and life as it was back home. There was gentleness in the way Kirat spoke. Like me, she was the youngest child. I could have loved her. I was attracted by her devotion. She had a soft voice – she sang holy songs at the gurdwara every Sunday.

Following her parents' wishes was quite natural for Kirat. We were allowed to be alone together with her sister-in-law acting as chaperone, in a badly-lit room. On the wall hung a print of the Tenth Guru. We sat opposite each other and I could tell from her eyes that she was attracted to me and I thought she was beautiful. We talked for about half an hour about what we did.

'I don't have a job,' I said. 'I've just graduated from college. I studied Philosophy. People don't think I'm a good prospect?'

'It doesn't bother me what people think, so long as you're a good person. People always gossip because they have little else to do. I don't like drama, but you get used to it when you're Indian. How do you feel about marriage?' she asked.

'I've never been in a situation like this. I think most marriages end up enslaving women and the woman comes to be seen as property. Why do you want to get married?'

'For me, marriage is an agreement to live and grow together, where two souls become one. It is a lifelong bond ordained by God. I believe that there's a time when every woman has to leave her parents' home. I'm ready to find a husband who I can love.'

'And what would you want from him?'

'Care and protection, I suppose.'

'Do you think I can give you that?'

'Yes.'

'But you don't know me.'

'I can see you're sensitive and maybe unsure about what's going on. Our parents are getting on really well. I'm certain if you give it a chance, we could be happy.'

'I like you. But I'm not sure if I'm ready to get married,' I said.

'What are your reasons?' she said.

'My family has many quarrels. I don't like what I see and I don't know if I could protect you. I just don't fit in.'

Kirat's sister-in-law spoke. 'Michael, every family has its own problems. When it comes to marriage what matters is the love that two people foster for each other. Love has to grow, it doesn't just appear. A man and woman have got get to know, trust and respect each other, everything else is of no importance. I feel you should marry. I'm saying this not just for Kirat, but you too. I feel it will be good for both of you.'

Kirat looked at me almost tearfully. 'Please say "Yes" to my proposal for marriage. I like you and I know we can make it work,' she said.

'I'll think about it,' I said.

For the first time my tradition, duty, and wanting freedom seemed to come together harmoniously. I wanted to embrace her. I sensed the promise of her being able to heal my wounds and save me from the passions loosened by my affair with Astrid. A clear inner voice counselled me to accept her. I would be marrying someone caring, but I couldn't help feeling fallen and dirty. I was searching for excuses to extricate myself from this arrangement, even though I believed it could save me.

We think we have free will; it is what makes us human, but I experienced it as a torture then. I was prepared to go against my conscience. In my mind, I concocted rationalisations to remove me from what my heart wanted. I thought my mother would be critical of her. Also, how could I explain to friends my reasons for having an arranged marriage when I had been such a romantic idealist? I felt that my arguments against marrying Kirat were shallow. I didn't want to grow up. Bitterness at having to take on responsibilities that I didn't want made me reject her. I resented my feeling that I needed to be forgiven for something, without knowing what I'd done wrong. I was a misfit who didn't want to play this game. I wasn't prepared to say sorry, so I forced myself to refuse this marriage.

A few days after returning from Coventry, my father told me that Kirat's family were waiting for a response from me. 'She's a kind, beautiful girl. I'd be so happy to have her as my daughter-in-law. Will you marry her?' he said.

'No, I can't,' I said.

'Why?'

'I don't feel ready. I feel unworthy.'

'This is nonsense. Please for my sake, accept her.'

'I'm so sorry. I can't.'

My father was hurt and angry at my decision. I was too proud to reconsider. I had betrayed him, severed myself from age-old tradition and entered a normless hinterland, which he saw as a path of self-destruction for me.

I was enveloped with self-loathing after refusing Kirat. My father became distant from me. He was unable to control his agitation, and whenever he had to talk to me, he wouldn't look at me. It was as if I had ceased to exist for him. At nights he'd come home tired and drunk and sleep without greeting my mother or me. All my extended family looked at me contemptuously. Only my mother's gaze was constant. I felt guilty for besmirching my father's reputation, and grief-stricken at being the cause of so much pain. Long silences weakened the intimacy between my parents and me. I wanted to walk away from the situation and say goodbye to the people who loved me.

One morning I woke up excited for no apparent reason. Without any plan in mind, I cycled to my dad's restaurant. I found him sitting in his customary place at a table in the corner. I sat down beside him, to feel close.

'Father,' I said, 'I am going to Paris to become a writer.' It was a spontaneous decision that had arisen from a childhood spent reading and writing poetry, and awakened by a middle school teacher who thought I would become a published author. His eyes were sad. He wished I wouldn't leave him but couldn't bring himself to prevent me from going after what had happened.

'When are you going?'

'Tomorrow morning.'

'So soon.'

'Yes.'

We kept the silence, looking at one another. I felt my heart racing. The time had come to leave my father's sanctuary and I was seeking his blessing.

'We were all young once,' he said. He smiled softly. Then he got up and poured two brandies, one for me and one for himself. We sat and drank the Cognac and it was a beautiful moment – the first and last time we ever had a drink together. I thought he was debonair and handsome like a 1950's film star.

A dull grey light diffused into the restaurant. We sat alone in the semi-darkness and I imbibed his sorrow at watching me grow, yet still remain young. He had been so gallant when he made his journey to Britain in the early 1960s, breaking with his own family's traditions and prohibitions. Now he was scared to let me go.

'Don't worry. I'll be back in six months,' I said.

Both of us knew that we would never see each other in the same light again.

I had taken to sending friends letters, writing down my intimate impressions of them. I wanted to reveal – especially to my closest friend Khalid, a Pakistani-British man in Cardiff, and Anarkali, the girl whom I had only observed from a distance – the way they figured in my imagination.

To Khalid, I spoke of the way in which his inner beauty animated the way he walked and talked and of his kindness that moved people to admire him.

I sent a letter for Anarkali's attention to her workplace. I wrote my fantasy of how I wished to play with her, chasing her naked through Bute Park beneath silvery moonbeams. I wrote that even though I would be turned on, I wouldn't make love to her. All I desired was to be free and share that liberation with her.

These portraits were a confession – a way of saying farewell in preparation for a life without them. She never replied, so I phoned her at her workplace one rainy day while out walking, from a phone box near the woods.

'Hi, it's Michael. I wrote to you. I hope I didn't offend you.'

Anarkali laughed. 'No,' she said. 'I enjoyed reading your letter. It was very brave of you. But you don't know me.'

'I know you, because I know myself.'

'But I've been with myself longer than you have.'

It was an enchanting reply that knocked me out and we arranged a rendezvous.

On the morning of taking the coach to Paris, I decided to secretly take a detour to see Khalid and Anarkali in Cardiff. My father hugged me in the courtyard of the coach station. I felt his warm cheek on mine. I loved him then with all my being. Then I bowed and touched his feet. I got onto the coach, my heart breaking. The buildings and streets and signs and hours began passing – I was lost in thought unaware even of where I was going. I had on my lap, a book I was reading. It was the Dhammapada, the Buddha's Path of Truth. Pages from it drifted in and out of the stream of my mind, and without even realising, Cardiff arrived and I found myself walking up St Mary's Street, beside Khalid, the autumn sun setting behind our backs.

PART TWO

1

Khalid was a lanky figure with a Roman nose that made him self-conscious. Both men and women received his openness as a sign of true friendship. There were times when he was pessimistic and expressed a barbed cynicism. As students, we had spent a lot of time drinking coffee at Rombout's watching people move through the busy sheltered arcade. This was the place where I passed him one evening while he was drunk, when he embraced me, declaring earnestly, 'I love you man!' I was touched and thereafter we became close.

Soon an evening spent without Khalid seemed empty to me. We met nearly every evening at his place with his housemates, with friends like Luke and Tyler often dropping in. We would often just sit around, sometimes smoking marijuana, while listening to music that slackened the longing we felt in our hearts to find something immeasurably great that withstood the onslaught of time. Nina Simone often did a turn, and we listened to Billie Holiday's mournful songs in silence, our heads bowed, eyes unfocused, gazing into the space between us. Sometimes we burst into reciting poetry from Rilke and Hafiz. Everyone was eager to show each other a fragment of their soul. We all wanted to unveil ourselves like artists.

Khalid was always keen for us to listen to John Cage, especially his rapturous setting of Psalm 19 where the skies and heavens are a tapestry, and creation is wrought word for word out of silence.

> The heavens are telling the glory of God:
> And the firmament proclaims his handiwork.
> Day to day pours forth speech,
> And night to night declares knowledge.
> There is no speech, nor are there words;
> Their voice is not heard;
> Yet their voice goes out through all the earth,
> And their words to the end of the world.

*

It had been a long journey, and though tired, I was happy to be with my friend. We sat in his living room above a pizza shop on City Road, reminiscing about the spring and golden summer we'd spent together. Our memories flowed easily, a record of Punjabi folk songs playing in the background. There was never a need to explain ourselves – there was always an immediate understanding between Khalid and myself that encompassed the whole fluid and complex nature of our identities. We were men who felt comfortable locating ourselves between places, languages, and ways of looking at the world. There was never a conflict between East and West. For us, rather, it was a heady blend of humanism and poetic insight. I always felt comfortable in Khalid's company. It seemed like we were reunited after many years as we looked into the crackling fire, which he'd lit earlier. Time moved like the notes plucked by a child on a violin. Khalid knew Anarkali and parts of her story gleaned from my talking about her. As he stoked the fire, he said, 'I envy you.'

'Don't say that,' I said.

'No, I mean it. I've become cynical since going out with Devi. I've tried to be free, but now find myself following the rules much like everyone else.'

'But you're already in love,' I said.

'It's not what you think,' he said. 'Being in love is when you can be completely alone with someone. I can't even be by myself or understand who I am, never mind Devi.'

The flames of the fire lit his face up. He looked a little forlorn. His usual self seemed shrouded by mundanity. I drank the wine and felt alone. Perhaps this really was the nature of the love, the mohabbat that Khalid was talking about, where time is inconsequential and one is entranced by the person in front, souls blend and the other becomes one's own axis mundi. My whole attention was completely focused on my friend. Yet, at the same time, I felt uneasy with the thought that I would have to leave soon.

'I have to go meet Anarkali,' I said. I felt like apologising.

'I'll drive you,' Khalid said.

He was relinquishing me to someone else. He was handing me over to the faintest possibility that perhaps I could realise my fantasy and be completely free while being devoted to a lover. We drove down the wet drizzly streets of City Road, strung with cheap takeaways and eateries past the crossroads called "Death Junction". My years of longing for Anarkali, were about to be put to rest. I wondered if she really could be like the person I imagined her to be, without ever really knowing her.

I got out of the car. 'See you later this evening,' I said.

'No need to rush. Enjoy paradise, my friend,' he replied.

I hurried to the place where I was supposed to be meeting Anarkali. I looked around the hall – a reggae band was playing a gig for a local charity, and then I saw this woman, who at first I didn't recognise, approaching me. Her long black hair that had formed such a strong part of her personality had been cut short, and she looked frailer than I remembered. She kissed my cheek and embraced me. It was as if we had known each other for many years, even though we had been separate for so long. I felt wounded as I stood holding her in the middle of the crowded space, unclear as to who was taking refuge in whom.

I had dreamt of being nude and chasing her through Bute Park under starlight. Now it felt as if I had caught a moist leaf falling in the autumn rain. Neither Anarkali nor I knew each other. We were both projections of the other's imagination. It was exciting and dangerous being so intimate with someone I had only seen from afar but was bound to remember for the rest of my life. The thin line between my perceptions and reality had been erased. At that moment, it felt like I was creating the world – the seasons, the cosmos, love and decay were all born out of my will. I was unafraid of death as it too was just an appearance in my dreamscape. I dived into her eyes and became lost in their loneliness. I prayed my mother and father forgive me, for having chosen a path that took me away from them to a place where absolution was now possible – only through Anarkali.

'How are you?' she asked.

'I'm good. I can't complain,' I said. 'I'm so glad to have met you at last.'

'Are you?' She was embarrassed. 'Shall we go somewhere?'

'I would love that.'

We walked into the night rain. The sky was huge. She entranced me. We walked into a club at the end of St Mary's Street called the Philharmonic. It was a real cattle joint. Men with their libidos on fire walked in on the prowl and women entered in groups desiring to be picked up. Everyone was getting drunk and rubbing up against each other. Downstairs, there was a cramped room called the "Bottleneck Bar" where a young woman sang Joni Mitchell covers. I used to come here sometimes after breaking up with Astrid, to listen to her renditions of songs that captured the zeitgeist of the late 1960s and 70s in her heartbreakingly beautiful voice, while the ceiling creaked and shook with the sound of pissed people dancing upstairs.

Anarkali and I stood holding hands like two children, clutching our bottles of beer, completely immersed in her singing, oblivious to the sexually charged scenes around us. We were inebriated with the alcohol and by the sprit of the sublime lyrics that spoke of blending people's souls together.

'Small talk is so painful,' Anarkali said. 'I can see that you don't like it. You don't give much away.' The music segued, faded in and out.

'I thought I was quite open,' I said.

'I didn't mean it as a criticism. I like it.' She put her head on my shoulder. 'I would like us to get to know each other better. Life has been so painful for me lately. You called me at a time when I really needed somebody.'

Anarkali became steadily drunk and began dancing by herself, her body willow-like, swaying to the music. Like many broken people whom I had encountered, she had been stripped of self-esteem. Her life didn't belong to her. Although she thought she was exercising a sovereign free will, everything she perceived and did was a reaction against attempts to control her.

'Can't you see you are dishonouring us? I want you to leave this house and never return,' her mother said, when Anarkali refused an arranged marriage.

'You're my parents. Where should I go?'

'You can go drown yourself in a river,' her father said.

Anarkali had been abandoned by her parents, brothers, and lovers. They tried controlling who she was and how she should behave; when she failed to conform, they treated her like an outcast. She had no choice except to become completely uprooted from her language and ignorant of where she belonged – who she was, how she was seen, and the chasm where she was headed. The way she was disowned wounded her being, which I sensed was momentarily soothed by one-night-stands and brief relationships. She was unaware until I told her that her name 'Anarkali' denoted the blossom of pomegranates.

We returned to her house around three in the morning. She made me coffee. I watched the dried powdered milk granules swirling aimlessly around the cup. I saw them as planets in constant revolution. Perhaps I thought I could read my fortune from the coffee grounds that remained in the cup. In my mind, there was no longer any disunion between the earthly and divine, the microcosm and the macro. It felt miraculous that love could be true and that someone had chosen to be with me for who I was. 'Look Anarkali, there are stars in my cup,' I said. I was beginning to find something deeply meaningful in everything small and insignificant. She smiled and we both looked at each other, giddy with how childlike we were being.

Anarkali led me by my hand to her bedroom, which was more of an artist's workshop. It was full of half-finished clay busts that were stacked on shelves and the various workbenches around the room. In a corner, there was a small table on which was placed the only complete figure. It was a sculpture of a woman that had been worked on intensely, since I could see the imprints of Anarkali's thumbs and fingers in the clay that gave the face an uneven and rugged texture. The eyes were cut deep and the nose was slender. There was something primordial about the head. Anarkali leaned over it, stroking the top with her hand. 'This is my mother,' she said. 'We don't talk anymore. Making this sculpture was the only way I could be near her.' She began crying. I watched her tears fall onto the clay bust and roll down. It was as if Anarkali was anointing and giving life to the mother for whom she was dead. We were both drunk and Anarakali took me to her single futon, which lay on the floor at the far end of the room. We lay down together, people who had found each other on the margins of our communities.

That night I dreamt uneasily of a valley surrounded by mountains on which there was a perpetual thunderstorm. On one side there appeared the head of a crone that repulsed me; on the other side was a magisterial sword emitting branches and I feared it. Then I heard a voice command me, 'Choose one,' but

I refused. Instead, I took the path through the middle that led to the mountains beyond. Every step was exhausting. This valley was untraversable. The terrain was strewn with the skeletons of people and beasts. There was no water to quench my thirst.

Anarkali woke me in the morning with croissants and fresh coffee that had a floral fragrance. 'I've decided to call in sick and take the day off work,' she said. I held her small hand, feeling its warmth and gentleness. She had opened up something inside me. My senses were enlivened to a timeless pain that must have been there even before the onset of my birth and the moment of separating from my mother. The room seemed palatial to me. I observed the rich paisley brocade on the thick curtains and the array of clay heads appeared to show an industrious person who began many things but was unable to finish them. There was also a self-portrait painted in acrylic on canvas that showed Anarkali with long hair looking morbid. When I got up, I saw Anarkali looking at my naked body and aroused sex. I felt ashamed and quickly took up the sheets to cover myself. 'You mustn't see me like this,' I said. 'I don't want you to think that I'm like every other man desiring you.'

'You're different,' she said, her head tilted slightly. 'I wouldn't have cried last night and we would have had sex if you weren't.'

I was hung-over, my head feeling dense. Her kindness was beginning to hurt. I didn't want this dreamlike situation to end but I needed a return to normality, where people relate to each other and talk in a mundane way, without meaning what they say. I wanted to dissolve the intensity of my concentration on our every word and movement. My vision scanned her body dressed in a Chinese gown and the vase of withered flowers beside her elbow. Was this a dream? Why did I feel so unusual and the world around me so unnatural? To me, it felt as if the world had disappeared and we were the last remaining people. I had fallen into a great silence and my senses were on hyperalert. I couldn't hear, feel or think in my accustomed manner amidst the usual traffic of ideas. Minutes seemed like hours and the quiet absorption in her beauty was beginning to disturb me. I desperately wanted to be outside in the open air. 'Anarkali,' I said. She was looking at me bemused by my shyness. 'I have to go out. I'll be back later in the afternoon and we'll go out together.'

'I'll get ready,' she said.

I walked out stunned by the morning light falling on my head. I couldn't feel the ground beneath me so I took off my shoes and felt the cool of the pavements and earth of the park on the soles of my feet. The refreshing air was enrapturing. I felt incredibly humble and thankful. Seagulls swept above me and in front, on a tall plinth was a statue of an angel holding an upright sword commemorating the dead of the great wars. Pity filled my heart as I could see thousands of dead bodies lying in fields smothered by the deafening sound of artillery and the green smoke of gas in my mind's eye. The memorial saddened me – the sword seemed to be calling out for more blood.

I began singing softly a Hindi melody. I was falling in love with everyone and everything. I greeted strangers passing with 'Good morning, brother' or 'Good morning, sister'.

My happiness and enjoyment of life was attracting kindness in return. 'You happy, love?' a woman called out.

'I'm very happy,' I said, swept up in a cloud of compassion.

My voice was sweet to listen to – I hadn't smoked too much. It rose and echoed off the tenements lining the street. My inner and outer worlds were in intimate praxis. I didn't care who recognised me, I was presenting the world with the gift of my joy. The song was from *Dosti*, one of my mother and father's favourite films. The title means 'Friendship':

I am the destiny of this miraculous world
I am a painting by the hands of the Father

I am a painting

I am wandering aimlessly from here to there

I am anxious

O passer-by look upon me, like you, I too am a human being [2]

At the same time, I was undergoing an internal interrogation. A sceptical voice in my brain asked me questions abrasively: 'What is the nature of life?'

'Love,' I said.

'Why is there suffering?'

I continued to sing choosing to ignore the rudeness of the tone of the questioner. I didn't want to get into a debate with it.

'Can love bring you food?'

'Yes,' I said.

'Can love bring you clothing?'

'Yes,' I said.

'Can love bring you shelter?'

'Yes,' I answered. 'I proclaim Love to be my God.'

Spontaneously, I become tearful now as I sit writing in my kitchen recalling those events, while some holy Sikh hymns are playing on YouTube in the background to help me relax. My attention is being drawn towards Salok Mahalla, 9 which was written by my Ninth Master, Guru Tegh Bahadur Ji, while he was in prison awaiting execution. I am moved by my guru's wisdom, gentleness, and immense love; they are like flowers which bloom even in the night, giving off their scent to heal souls that have been afflicted by grief. The Ninth Guru gave himself up with complete humility, to be tortured and martyred so that all people could freely practise their own religion without fear of persecution.

This hymn is usually recited at someone's passing from this life. The words stir my emotions, making them swell and contract with the heaving of my lungs. Interlaced within this spiritual–physical web is the memory from all those years ago when I first lost my mind, drifting along Queen Street in Cardiff, feeling triumphant, playing with children making them laugh and babble. Their mothers blushed with the attention I gave them and their babies. My wanting Anarkali had transformed. She'd become the wood fuelling the fire of my desire to come face to face with my creator. Anarkali had seduced me to metamorphose into a moth and annihilate myself at the apex of an ageless flame. The Guru sings in his hymn:

> You must know this world is like a dream, a show
> Nothing inside it, is true without God
> Night and Day a mortal wanders endlessly
> For the sake of Maya.
> Amongst millions scarcely anyone keeps the Lord in his
> Consciousness

I kept looking towards the sun. It seemed to be rising constantly and becoming brighter. The day felt like it was getting longer and there would be no ending to it. Even in the middle of crowds, I was alone. The world was empty. Fear crossed my mind. I began to sense that I was behaving strangely and couldn't grasp the person I habitually was. Then Khalid appeared walking down the steps of the university students' union looking radiant with his truth and goodness. We flung our arms around each other. 'Allah Hu Akbar,' I shouted, pointing towards the sky. Although Khalid had been born into a Muslim family, his immersion in science had led him to abandon any belief in God and he now pronounced himself an atheist. I suppose out of embarrassed politeness, he greeted me with, 'Sat Sri Akal.'

'Khalid,' I said. 'Let's spend the afternoon together.'

'Let's do that, man,' he said.

I cannot forget the day when I broke down. In hindsight, my psychosis had been budding for some time, but beneath the intense autumn sunshine streaming down from an azure sky, it fully blossomed.

Khalid and I did an exhausting tour of the city. We later called it our "walkabout". I kept pointing to trees and naming them. I imagined I was Adam at the beginning of time speaking anew the words pregnant with the reality of things in paradise. An amazing joy coursed through my body. I felt invincible. My battered faith had been revived. From the ground, I began collecting stones, leaves, twigs, and pieces of broken glass. As for a child, these unwanted objects became precious talismanic trinkets to aid my incarnation in this world.

'Look,' said Khalid, 'they're painting Gwyneth's room.' She had been a friend of ours who had committed suicide a year before. We stopped in a reverential moment looking up at the workers stripping the walls that she had once adorned with postcards of paintings by artists like Cezanne and Modigliani. One had been of Picasso's *La Vie* from his Blue Period set in his studio. It shows a naked couple keeping at arm's length Picasso's mother who is carrying a child in her arms. In the background, there are two paintings of vulnerable people in the nude, captured in various degrees of trauma and distress. This had been Gwyneth's homage to the art that lifted her out of the torment she concealed. Khalid hid his face. I put my arm around him to comfort him.

I was in what felt like immediate contact with reality. I was on the fringes of what could be expressed in language. There was no separation between my perceptions and the objects of my perception. I felt in complete union with the world. I was experiencing my life with all my senses, directly without a mediating Ego. I was the leaf that I sang about, clinging to a tree. I was that tree that had matured and gleaned its wisdom over centuries.

*

I am beside Khalid; we are moving forward together even though we are still and the world is moving through us. We are oblivious of the time or where we are headed, unafraid that this might be the last day we are alive. Khalid and I intuitively know we are of the same spirit yet so different and so apart. Death cannot vanquish us with this condition of knowledge. We are two boys walking out of the chamber of our mother's womb.

2

We bought bottles of Veuve Clicquot champagne. The shopkeeper was so infected by our pleasure that he happily gave us three glasses for free. We strode though the market and stopped at a flower stall. I began creating my own bouquet of flowers by picking each stem carefully for its beauty and scent. Khalid and the florist watched, entertained by my seemingly unending work. My bouquet was an embodiment of contrast and harmony, flowers coming together while clashing in their profusion of colours, tones and fragrances. I felt proud and empowered holding the bouquet and carrying it through the market, as if it was my machine gun.

We arrived at Anarkali's house late in the afternoon.

'So you decided to come at last,' she said.

I handed her the flowers smiling broadly. 'This is Khalid,' I said.

'Pleased to meet you,' she said.

'We've met before – a long time ago. I wouldn't expect you to remember,' Khalid said.

Then we all embraced each other as if we had been long-lost siblings.

'Let's go somewhere. It's so beautiful,' I said.

'I don't mind going to the sea, so long as you drive,' Anarkali said.

'But I don't have a car,' I replied.

'You can drive mine,' she said.

'I can't drive.'

'Don't worry. I'll drive if you don't mind,' Khalid said.

We got into Anarkali's old red Volkswagen and drove for miles with the windows wound down. I sat at the back, while my friends talked with each other at the front. I stuck my head out of the window and whooped for joy, feeling the wind rushing through my hair. We were alive and this was all that mattered. Sometimes I just closed my eyes concentrating on the cold freshness engulfing my face. The car stereo was playing music but for me the whole cosmos had become a song.

When we got to the sea, we sat on the rocks, drinking and listening meditatively to the waves crashing in on each other. The sea's vastness reached out to the horizon where the sun was blending in with the clouds. God, the source of my peace and solace in my pain, had awoken auspiciously in the world. Prayers kept fluttering in my mind. The universe had appeared and would disappear again and I was humbled that I could know this. I held Anarkali's hand softly knowing that this unexpected dream would end.

'I'm scared I'll lose you,' I said.

'You're not going to lose me. You've rescued me. Now stop being so melancholic.' A tear clung to her eyelashes. 'We're so bloody melodramatic, aren't we?' she said.

The onset of my madness was as sudden or as slow as the opening of a dandelion at dawn. In my insanity, I became auto-religious. I could not stop praising the Divine. Everywhere I turned, in everything, I sensed His presence. All three of us were gods enjoying our work. The fragrance of the champagne suffused the air. I drank greedily tasting every drop, then in an angry, despairing act of trying to sever myself from my past, I smashed my empty glass and watched the ocean swallow the debris. I concentrated on the waves lapping up the shattered pieces. Nothing remained of my identity – I had lost my home, parents, and culture. These two friends were everything to me at that moment but somewhere unconsciously I missed my mother, I missed my father and I missed me.

The pinkish streetlights turned on and the traffic eased. We drove easily down the roads. I was lost in an ecstatic reverie. I kept wanting to look at Anarkali's eyes in the rear-view mirror. What did they see in me? How could she love me, a fallen creature? I thought.

We got back late into a quiet city. I didn't feel at all present in my body.

'I'll see you tomorrow,' Anarkali said, her eyes gleaming. Without saying it, she was committing herself to me.

'Will we meet again?' I asked feeling anxious. Perhaps this was the perfect moment to let go – not a single argument, nothing boring, only the intensity of the universe showing itself in its symbolic dress. I had become enamoured with Anarkali and she had given me the gift of encountering my life afresh. I was observing her, Khalid, and myself struck with wonderment as if we had just emerged from a fragrant olive grove.

Khalid and I returned to his flat. He was overwhelmed by what was happening to me. I was drunk on either life or the alcohol – I couldn't keep my balance, so he carried me upstairs, a little like a bride being taken to bed. I was unable to sleep, on the lookout for any sound or movement to distract myself. It was oppressively peaceful. I didn't want to be a burden, I wanted to be somewhere where I could be completely alone, so I crept out of the house and stepped into the cold night.

My rational mind had ceased functioning. I had no notion of where I was, nothing was recognisable, I was lost but still unafraid. I was following my feet in whichever direction they took me, functioning completely on instinct. I eventually came across a graveyard where I thought I could rest. I crouched beneath a tree looking at the burial places. The poetry and verses from the Bible on the gravestones revealed nothing about the history of the interred beings, whose end they marked. 'What am I doing here?' I asked myself.

At last it seemed that I was alone, which should have given me some comfort, but I was restless. I began feeling there was something uncanny present in the silence. I got up and began walking fast along a path encircling the graveyard, then broke out running through the pitch darkness. I tripped and fell. The madness had taken hold of me completely. On my knees, I began kissing the graves trying to awaken the dead inside them and the one who had died inside me. The dirt and gravel on my lips felt good. My mind was split in two, something was seriously wrong, but I could not help being completely immersed in an epic play that was no longer pretend; a divine game in which I was being compelled to participate in and enjoy.

'Please, God,' I shouted. 'What's happening to me?'

From out of nowhere, I heard an angel's voice speak to me. 'Don't be afraid,' it said, 'Go forward and meet the Devil.'

I had lost my sanity. It was terrifying. I had crossed the limits of my mind and found myself sick and lost. Trembling, I got up and started walking forward to discover what lurked in the darkness. There was a wall of energy drawing me towards itself. Misshapen animals began appearing out of the darkness and then reentering it. I couldn't distinguish whether they were real or imagined; I was hallucinating. I tried closing my eyes but had no control – some sort of latent courage and curiosity made me continue looking even more intently at the apparitions. I was frightened. Then a horrible subhuman visage materialised. It lacked a body and its cadaverous flesh seemed to melt into the air becoming invisible with the night. The Devil had appeared – he was the darkest, most vile aspect of my own humanity projected across this graveyard. Revulsion awakened in me. I began mourning and through the tears I was horrified to see the Devil's face metamorphose into nothing other than my own reflection. My own self was looking back at me. Everything I found revolting in my psyche, the immoral subterranean desires and conniving voices had all been set rampantly free, accusing me of having built a comfortable persona by repressing and murdering them. Sickness exhausted me, words ceased to mean anything and lay like shards of a broken mirror on the floor of my brain. I collapsed onto the ground. I waited, trembling like a panic-stricken creature for the night to end and the sun to rise.

It began getting lighter. A quarter moon still clung to the sky and shone through the twisted branches of trees in silhouette. I got out of the graveyard at dawn, the empty streets were lined with black bin bags ready for collection. There was a pile of old clothes and I remembered the interrogating voice which had asked me, 'Can love bring you clothing?'

'Yes,' I said to myself. 'Love can bring you clothing.' Impulsively, I took off my clothes in the street and put on the discarded garments. I looked like a depressed tramp. A milkman was on his deliveries. He was a compassionate man who must have sensed that I was thirsty and hungry and, out of kindness, he gave me a bottle of milk. I felt jubilant. 'Look,' I said to myself. 'Love can bring you food.' I drank some of the milk, I poured some on my head and washed my face with it. With the rest of the milk, I drew a circle on the ground, as a propitiatory offering to the gods, then smashed the bottle. I began dancing on the broken glass, for Shiva the Destroyer, in thanks for giving me life. I felt so touched by the Divine, I danced uncaring about the pain I felt, my blood staining the road. All that was needed now was a shelter, a place of sanctuary for my truth to be vindicated that love can bring you everything.

Close by was a church. I entered the grounds where there was a white statue of Mother Mary. She wore a golden crown and smiled serenely. In her lap played the baby Jesus. I prostrated myself sobbing uncontrollably hugging the base of the statue with my bloodied feet. 'Please, Mother,' I said. 'I can't carry on like this. I want to return home.' I lay there for a long time. Eventually a priest dressed in a black cassock came out clearly disgusted by my down-and-out appearance gesturing wildly with his arms saying, 'Shoo! Shoo!' I turned away alarmed and ran out of the church grounds.

I have no idea how I found my way back to her house. Anarkali held back her tears and Khalid who she had called over to help, looked uncomprehendingly as to what was happening to me. I wasn't talking, because it was too much of an effort. At that moment, words seemed futile in communicating the onslaught of thoughts and sensations I was experiencing; they denoted nothing. Language had become an imperfect mirror for the kaleidoscopic. Truth that had come alive in my awakening soul. Anarkali was bewildered by my behaviour. She couldn't have known whether to laugh at my idiocy or be in awe of the tragedy that was unfolding. For Khalid, it was clear; I needed psychiatric help. They took me to Whitchurch Mental Hospital.

Two doctors were present to assess me. They looked concerned but I said nothing to the dismal automatic questions they asked:

'Do you hear voices?'

'Do you think you are someone you are not?'

'Do you believe you are being watched?'

'Do you think your identity is being stolen from you?'

Eventually one of the doctors asked, 'Can you spell the word "world"?'

'W o r l d,' I said.

'Now can you spell it backwards?'

I struggled and understood I couldn't. I was annoyed with

myself. I realised I was in trouble and that I too wanted to rescue my rational faculty which had disintegrated because of fear, loss, and sorrow.

It was decided that for my own safety and for the protection of the public I should be detained at the hospital. Anarkali, Khalid, and I held hands and skipped down the long corridors leading to the ward singing, 'We're off to see the Wizard, the wonderful Wizard of Oz.' Though we were exuberant, it was a surreal and pathetic scene.

I was so trammelled and dirty when I arrived in Ward E53 that the first thing a nurse called Janet did was to take me to the bathroom. I playfully took off the old rags and got into the warm foamy bath she had run for me. At last I had found shelter. 'Om Shanti Om, Waheguru, Waheguru,' I intoned, pouring water from a plastic beaker onto my head in relieved thanks. Janet's hair was tied up in a bun, highlighting her high cheekbones. She looked like a painting by Vermeer, so beautiful, sitting on a chair watching me bathe. The natural light from the large window penetrated the steam as it rolled off in clouds from the surface of the water. I looked at my carer and felt deeply indebted for her kindness.

3

I stood looking at my reflection in the ceiling-to-floor windows of ward E53. It was a damp afternoon. Trees were in conflagrant autumn colours; leaves were blowing across the grass. It felt special being the only patient detained in the large secure ward of this labyrinthine Victorian mental hospital, a complex of dark jutting towers and chimneys, with long intersecting corridors, rooms with bolted metal doors from which so many inmates had recently been released to find their own way in the oppressive world outside.

*

I was twenty-three. I had been sectioned with my first psychotic breakdown. It was September 1992. The Care in the Community Act was being implemented. Long-time mental patients, who had been imprisoned in often eerie gothic hospitals, were being released back into the lap of their communities, ending decades of ignominy. For many of the mentally vulnerable and impaired it was a fearful time. Leaving the familiar sanctuary of the places where they had lived an institutionalised life with friends (real and imagined), they heaved a sigh of unfettered freedom stepping out to meet the indifference of the public.

As circumstances go, I had been a fish swimming against the current. I was too ill to be left outside. I had fallen in love with a woman who loved me. Her generous act of reciprocity made me feel as if the sun, planets and stars had aligned for just a moment in celebration of our communion. Everything felt in symphonic harmony.

The few days I spent with Anarkali had been sensual. The synergy created by our meeting, had put me in awe of even the simplest objects. I had awakened to a world saturated with meaning: random stones on the ground appeared to be so precious, the surgical instruments in the hospital used to tear into the brains of patients were divine sculpting tools and the paisley pattern woven into the carpet described the movement of the Milky Way. Before being doped up on drugs like diazepam, I loved this Earth with my entire being and I'd felt overjoyed without limit at the presence of what I perceived was the sacred in life.

I am still unsure if the catalyst to drive me insane was Anarkali's seductive beauty or the painful feelings of being rejected by previous lovers like Astrid. But I was thrown by an inner passion, towards seeing a transcendent god in every living thing. Nothing was more precious than this life. The divine soul was animate and poured out as light from people I observed passing by. I loved one and all including the terrier who sensing my disconnectedness began pulling on his leash, yapping at me. I was in a rapture. My consciousness had been sucked into the world around me. I was certain that the concrete and steel of the cityscape to the tarmac on which I tread contained God.

But this overpowering feeling degenerated into turmoil. Paradoxically, I reasoned that if God was alive here and now in this world then how could he possibly exist? Heaven was empty. I became terrified by the void left by the absence of there being an immortal transcendent being, by the lack of an indomitable destroyer of the filth of this world. The anguished disunion between Anarkali and me was killing and I longed to bury my head in my mother and father's bosom to sob. I was small, afraid and lonely in E53. Afflicted with insomnia, I'd lie on the lumpy mattress of my hospital bed devoid of hope, too scared to acknowledge the fact that in my imagination I had already died.

In my state of madness, I was fixated with the belief that our souls are imperishable. Before blossoming in our mother's womb, the world is experienced by us as a faint indecipherable dream. Every breath inhaled is exhaled like a silent elegy to oneself. My being was completely open to life. In that state, I thought I could sense a seed being borne in the air on a spring breeze, millions of people bleeding and dead in forgotten wars, the morning flight of birds across roaring oceans. This was what it was like. Imagine yourself in a space before being born – in that immeasurable emptiness, everything is cast inside the visceral darkness of the heart and in the light of the mind – it is here that an androgynous God lives enjoying creation's dance. It was enough to make me weep.

*

I never made it to Paris. The night before being incarcerated, I called my mother from a phone box that smelt of stale urine with Anarkali standing beside me.

'Peri Pena,' I said, greeting her in a polite yet loving Indian manner, as a way of showing my veneration.

'May you live a long life, Michael,' she said.

'How are you?'

'I'm good. You've only been gone two days. I'm missing you. Your father is upset. He's not angry. You are so far away. We wish you would come back home.'

'I can't do that,' I said tightening my hand around Anarkali's. 'I've found someone. I hope you'll meet her soon. I feel I've grown up. I feel ready to fly from my birdcage.'

I was happy with my declaration of freedom. For years, I had become withdrawn from my mother, since I experienced her needing me as overwhelmingly restrictive. It was the first time I was confiding something intimate to her. The night was starry and felt just like the painting by Van Gogh. I had been too afraid to challenge my mother's over protectiveness until this spontaneous outpouring and emotionally too unaware about why I had been afraid of betraying her.

'What's her name, Michael?' my mother asked, her voice affected with softness.

'Anarkali,' I said.

'That's a beautiful name. Is she the right person for you?'

'I am sure she is,' I said.

4

I am lying in a hospital bed, surrounded by people. There is Dr Edwards, a consultant psychiatrist at the hospital. He's a kind bespectacled man with a white beard. Alongside him are Dr Moyle, who is sweaty and twitching nervously because he is new to his position, Janet, and another nurse whose name is Robert – both of them have been on constant watch, observing and reporting on my condition. It's late evening and they're concerned for me because I haven't slept for three nights and my behaviour is increasingly agitated.

I feel as if I have died a long time ago, but my spirit doesn't want to leave this earthly realm. I am dead. I am acting dead. At first, I think the psychiatric staff are supernatural beings, sort of angels, counselling me to enter into the light of an afterlife. I am observing things from outside myself. I am wonderstruck at the gracefulness of our human form: the beauty of our muscular bodies that have been evolving since the beginning of time to reach such perfection in the relationship between limbs, torso, and head. Everything appears calm but beneath the surface there is torment. Soon, the scene sinks into delirium. I don't wish to leave this life. I want to remain here. I might be hallucinating, but suddenly ugliness descends on me and upon those in whose care I have been placed. The situation is like the madness depicted in a painting by Hieronymus Bosch: people and animals behaving orgiastically, in a timeless unlit penumbra. Dr Edwards, the consultant, is down on his knees looking at me with dilated eyes as if in adoration. Janet has strapped my arm and Dr Moyle is injecting a syringe full of haloperidol into it. Khalid is present. I am pleading with him: 'Take me out of here. Please take me home.' Khalid is full of remorse. He doesn't understand. I think he's part of a conspiracy to finish me off. I am weary from the unending parade of thoughts clashing in my brain and begin falling into a slumber. I want to die but then I don't. I want to be alone and not surrounded by the spirits of people who have never lived.

*

Every so often, one of the nurses came and looked in through the porthole window of my secure room. A dull yellow bulb was kept on all night since I was afraid of the dark. I wasn't at all sure what demons the bars on the windows were meant to be keeping out. It was a terrible sleep filled with the appearances of archetypes and mythical monsters. Chief amongst the apparitions was the Tibetan Buddhist figure Mahakala standing on a field of corpses, wearing a crown of skulls. His mask was grotesque and I shook with fear. I mistook him for something evil whereas he is the protector of compassion, dispensing with his sword the degeneracy and dross of an ill-spent unethical life. I yearned in my delirium for my mother. I could sense the closeness of her delicate face and derived comfort from it. 'There's nothing to be afraid of my child,' she said. Then my mother was superseded by a troupe of angelic women with porcelain skin whose kisses I thought would devour me and I was ashamed, unable to control my sexual desire. In the midst of my psychodrama, every forbidden passion was let loose and its physical manifestation was a persistent erection. My world had been bolted open by an awakening of love, but I could not endure the pain of knowing everything is subject to decay. Above my head, a round dusty paper lightshade swung gently in a draft and I became fixated with the hallucination that I was a foetus seeking warmth wrapped around that dull bulb.

I woke up in the middle of the night and tried looking at my reflection in the mirror. I didn't know the person staring back at me. I tried observing myself from different angles, contorting my face in different ways, trying to mould the figure that best represented me when my rationality was intact – these eyes, lips, nose, and face were not mine. This body did not belong to me, it was the remains of some other being. Tired of trying to find myself, I slipped back onto the bed. Someone was trying to cry but it was not me. At last, I slept face down. My brain had stopped thinking and retracted into emptiness.

The morning light streamed into E53. The door of my room was unlocked. I walked into the desolate ward and sat alone at a row of long tables. Waiting outside, I saw that there were auburn trees touched by the fresh sun and that the dew was heavy – the grass appeared so lush. The medication had begun to work, deadening my senses and reducing me into a remote shadow of what I had been. How different my mood was only hours before when I happily embraced my madness and skipped down the hospital's long corridors hand-in-hand with Khalid and the woman we loved, singing. Now my soul felt desperately sad, my surroundings were of no interest to me, nor did I care for myself. The fuse that had animated my life hitherto seemed to have been snuffed out. I wondered why I was the only one on this ward.

But in that long empty room, I was content to think of it as a period of penance for having momentarily believed I was God. I felt I had seen Him somewhere, but I could not distinguish anymore between dream and reality. I sat fidgeting with my hands, my expression blank. My feeling miserable was made worse because I could hear someone hammering and I connected it with the thought that Christ had reincarnated again and again since Golgotha. The Second Coming had already taken place many times, but repeatedly out of fear of losing our own power we refused to acknowledge him and consistently nailed him to the cross.

Loneliness in E53 was killing me. I played table tennis for hours every day by myself against the other side of the table, which had been turned up. The hard, methodical tapping of the ball hitting the wood echoing around the room soothed me. An African-Caribbean man came to clean the ward. I would watch him work, listening to the slap of his mop as he washed the grey linoleum floor. A bright wet patch would appear beneath every swish of the mop. Beads of sweat gathered across this gentle man's creased brow like a string of pearls. I listened to a lot of music on the radio and smoked. Khalid visited me in the evenings, bringing with him curry he had cooked at home. He'd watch me gulping down my meal with my fingers, as if I hadn't eaten in days.

'How's Anarkali?' I said mid–mouthful.

'She's alright. She's getting on with her life,' Khalid said.

'Do you think she loves me?'

'I don't know. Your priority should be to get better.' Khalid was avoiding being honest. Deep down, he was confused and angry with the worry my illness had caused him and everyone around me.

David, my first co-patient, was brought onto the ward mid-afternoon after I had been there alone for about nine days. He was a beautiful man, tall, slim, and in his early twenties with short-cropped hair. We immediately liked each other despite hardly talking. He was gay and HIV-positive. He had suffered from routine insults and homophobia in the cramped Rhondda Valley town from where he came. News that he was incurably ill brought up all the fire-and-brimstone rubbish and 'just punishment for his perversions' stuff from his chapel-going family. Everyone except his ageing mother disowned him. David had sunk into a low depression, refusing to bathe, cut his nails or leave the hostel where he lived with addicts, drunks, and people and families with nowhere else to go. As well as dejection and despair, the place brimmed with aggression and he began getting into violent confrontations. He found himself bullied, but the aggressors became afraid and backed off when David would show his long fingernails and tell the bastards that he would infect them with AIDS. He began enjoying his newfound power because he was threatening anyone who so much as looked upon him with disgust. His senses had become attuned to the harshness of the world and he intimately trusted his instincts. His social workers thought he was paranoid and had him committed on the grounds of being a danger to others.

I don't know how long we've been together or how we even came to be friends.

David and I sit and eat together.

Sometimes, he asks me, 'Mike, what ya doin' here? Are you a sort o' psychopath?'

'I don't know,' I reply. 'I guess like you, I just have to be here.'

'Were you on too much wacky backy?' he says.

'No,' I said. 'I just fell in love. That's all.'

The two of us used go to the nurses' room to take our medication. Then we would dance for hours in the ward to the latest songs on the radio. Our favourite – or at least the one that I think was being played specially for me – was Bob Marley singing 'I'm Getting Iron Like a Lion in Zion'. The nurses sometimes gathered around us smiling, clapping rhythmically, watching as we whirled like dervishes. It was a retreat from the absurdity of the world. The TV would be on low volume, and the unemotive news and documentaries showed the continuing aftermath of the Gulf War. The oil fields of Kuwait were still burning; soldiers were suffering from Gulf War Syndrome; there was starvation on the streets of Baghdad, where the regime had become even more repugnant. The pictures on the TV screen displayed a world beset by unending carnage and crisis, even though the Cold War was officially over, and the old communist countries of Europe were being dismantled. For David and me in E53, the news images on the TV betokened another time and space. We were glad to be in this prison locked away from the world and its despicableness.

5

I had been in E53 for a month when I allowed the psychiatric nurses to contact my parents and inform them of my condition. I had been worried about how my psychotic breakdown would be communicated to them, as they spoke no English. Eventually Janet, the nurse whom I had grown to trust, phoned my dad's restaurant and my middle brother translated to my father that I was very sick.

My father visited me with my mother, who was wearing black NHS sunglasses to block out the light because of an operation she had had to remove a cataract. My brother-in-law, Josh, had driven them down from Leeds. He wore a black bomber jacket emblazoned on the back in gold embroidery with the Sikh insignia of the Khanda, showing two swords that enable a person to fight oppression and also discern Truth from Untruth. He walked around the table tennis-table, emitting solidity and strength, smiling to see me looking so sheepish. 'You're not mad,' he said, in his West Midlands brogue. 'Losin' your mind can be sign of true love. I hope she's good-looking.'

'She is,' I said.

'She must be special for you to be in such a state.'

'He's ill,' my father said, his voice emotional and critical. 'How can he know if she's good for him?'

'Does she want you?' asked Josh.

'I haven't seen her. I don't know what she wants.'

'Good job. You look really terrible.' I laughed. 'Don't think too much,' Josh said. 'I'm here to help. You only need to ask.'

'I know,' I said.

I hadn't smiled in a long time and sat with them silently, feeling hopeful, and protected. All three of them had been a strong presence in my life. Seeing them now felt like a partial return to normality. My mother brushed my uncombed hair, then held my face between her hands and kissed my forehead. 'I consulted an astrologer when I heard you were sick. He said, 'Everything is going to be fine. He'll get better.' Waheguru will protect you, my son.' Her voice was emotional – a tear rolled down from behind her glasses. My father was more reserved. He was walking around the room, unable to keep still, looking sad and thoughtful. It had been painful for him when I rejected the arranged marriage with Kirat. Now he felt remorseful that his favourite child, who he thought would accomplish great things, had been incarcerated in a mental hospital.

'They told me you were sick and have to be on medication for the rest of your life. This is not a hospital. It's a prison,' he said.

I had wanted to make him proud of me and show him that I could overcome the caste system in a way that didn't hurt and dishonour anyone. The drugs had turned me into a spiritless mannequin and I had failed in my own eyes, if not in his. Were it not for a vain hope of being with Anarkali, perhaps I would have listened more receptively or even submitted to the vicious voice urging self-annihilation: *I've lost my mind. I've lost the person I love. I've disrespected my parents. I'm of no use to society. What point is there in remaining alive?*

While we sat together in E53 late into the funereal afternoon, I sang quietly part of a Sikh psalm, which was like an analgesic for my loved ones and healing for my psychological wounds. The words made me emotional and my father wanted to know why I was crying. My mother wiped my face tenderly as my voice quivered: 'Mera Mujh Mein Kich Nahin...'

I have nothing inside me.
Whatever there is, is Yours.
By returning to You your gifts
What remains that I can possibly call my own?

Trying to unburden myself of what did not belong to me had cost me dearly. I wished I had obeyed my father. I wished for my mother to birth me again so that I might repeat my life – but that was impossible. I did not feel beautiful and, deep down, I lamented my being born. A few days after they left, I asked for a priest to come and visit me in E53. He was a tall elderly man who wore a black cassock and red skullcap. He asked us to pray. He laid his hand on my head. We said the Lord's Prayer together. 'God bless you, my son,' he said at the end and then left.

*

The days in E53 are long. David worries about me. When we are not making merry dancing, we sit looking out of the windows. Though feeling protected and fearing the outside world, there is a longing to be free and experience the mundanities of life, like going to the local shops and carrying home the groceries in blue plastic bags or just shooting some pool in a local pub, having set aside our internal conflicts and worries. 'Mike,' he says. 'P'rhaps we can find a place together when we get outta here.'

'I would like that. But what would we do?' I say.

'Man, we'd enjoy ourselves just like we do now.'

'It wouldn't be the same, David.'

'You're so earnest. Can't we just dream for a moment? Let's allow our minds to be free. I need to act, to feel the blood pump through my veins and say that I'm alive. Being in here with you is wonderful, but it's an escape from the hardness and beauty that can be life.'

I knew David was right. But my life was devoid of hope.

I tried talking to Anarkali from the payphone on the ward.

'Hello, it's me.'

'I know it is. What do you want?' Her voice was stern.

'I just wanted to talk. I missed you and wish you would come and visit me.' There was a long silence. I continued, 'I'm getting better. They've put me on tablets that will cure me...'

'I'm glad. You're sounding more like yourself.' Her unsympathetic words sounded empty. She was humouring me when I needed a sense of warmth. I was beginning to anticipate the sounds of the pips going indicating that my money had run out.

'Anarkali, will you call me back?' I asked.

'No, I'd rather not. I'm too busy,' she said.

'Will you visit me?'

'Not sure.'

6

David has no visitors in E53. He is jealous and protective of his friendship with me. He believes that Khalid and Anarkali betrayed me by having me sectioned. Had he been in their place, he would never have brought me into this asylum. We understand each other: neither of us believe we are really psychotic. We are the detritus of society's shameful inability to value individuals intrinsically for who they are but we are empathic beyond reason with the purpose of everyone's existence. Amnesia is afflicting people's intuition about what intimacy, care, and love really mean. A deep forgetting hangs over civilisation concerning what makes us human – we have consented to become functionaries of a sterile system in which all relations are reduced to a utility and monetary exchange value. It is a state where greed prevails consuming all that is good, co-opting, and perverting the noble values underpinning beautiful humanity.

David is smoking, his bruised fingers clutching the cigarette tightly, his eyes looking at the smoke circles floating languorously up towards the ceiling. He wants to save me. He knows I am scared of Sam who has just come onto the ward. I fear Sam because he is completely irrational – he's young and fat with a foul body odour that overwhelms me. Sam's a trainee doctor who enjoys aggression. He needs to be in control especially over vulnerable people. He punched one of his patients, an old woman. Instead of going to prison, he claimed diminished responsibility. I am weaker than him and there is nothing more he would like than to beat the living daylights out of me.

*

One day, Gillian the occupational therapist arrived with a black eye. I asked her how she got it. She looked nervous. 'I had a fall,' she said. It was obvious someone had punched her. We sat drawing, around a table in E53.

Sam kept staring at Gillian lecherously. 'Did your boyfriend do that to you?' he said, enjoying her looking painfully uncomfortable.

'Shurrup,' David said. 'If you want to pick on somebody, start with me.' Sam smiled, his expression full of contempt. David got up, pushing his chair back.

'I wouldn't try anything, if I were you,' Sam said, 'You'll be in here for the rest of your life. My dad's a justice of the peace.'

'I don't care about what anybody can do to me.' David began to circle the room, a predatory animal looking for the kill, his eyes full of menace. The gentleness that he often exuded had vanished; he was completely transformed. Gillian was anxious. She ran to the door to summon help. David turned over the table which came crashing onto the floor. He was about to lunge at Sam, intent on scarring him with his nails, when the nurses rushed in, but their sudden appearance exacerbated his distress. He tore off his shirt as the nurses tried holding him and then whipped around shouting, 'I'm gonna kill you, I'm gonna kill you, you evil bastard.' Sam, who was on his feet seemed only a little afraid, and he laughed mockingly, hiding behind one of the nurses.

I went into David's room. He was curled up on his bed looking at the wall. 'Are you alright?' I said.

'Yeah.'

'You don't look so good.'

'You're hardly an oil paintin' yourself,' he said.

I tried smiling but the haloperidol paralysed my mouth. I was proud he was my friend. David had been spoiling for a fight with Sam. When Sam was humiliating Gillian, it had been a convenient trigger for David to unleash his anger.

'Thanks for protecting me,' I said, 'If it weren't for you, I think I would have given up.'

Then it occurred to me that David wasn't on medication. His expressions and way of talking were fluid whereas I struggled, my speech slurred, my tongue salivating like a dog's, trembling from the effects of the chlorpromazine.

'There's nothing to be afraid of except your own shame and guilt,' David said.

'What do you mean?'

'Are you scared of me?'

'No.'

'Then do you pity me? What is it? Because I'm not gettin' anything from you.'

'What do you want?' I asked.

'Nothing except friendship. But you're afraid of me. You're afraid of being intimate and that's the reason you became sick.'

I stood feeling downhearted, unable to respond. David was regretful and from sympathy he reached out to embrace me. I shrunk under the lightness of his arms. I didn't want anyone to come close to my body, because I found it grotesque – it had its own desires separate from my mind, the sensations that I felt on my skin aroused incomprehension.

7

Dr Edwards is eating his lunch. 'What's wrong with me?' I ask him.

'We don't know,' he replies.

'So why I am here?' I say.

'You suffered from an acute psychosis of an unknown origin.' The words have an authoritative quality – they signify nothing, but their form is the justification for my being interned in this institution.

'How long will I have to remain on the medication?'

'What happened was very serious, Michael. You had lost control of your thoughts and were possibly hallucinating. We are not sure of the causes, but the psychosis is likely to recur. Anything stressful like a broken relationship, death in the family, travelling, can be a trigger. It's likely that you should be on medication for long time.'

'How long is that?'

'Maybe the next twenty or twenty-five years on lithium.'

I was being pronounced sick for the rest of my life. I felt dismayed that science, which can't even distinguish between the mind from the body and is unable to cure so-called 'mental illness', had thrown me onto a trash heap. Dr Edwards seemed like a nice man, with my best interests at heart, but I disliked the way he made his solemn pronouncement munching a ham-and-cheese sandwich. It was absurd and even more painful that he didn't have the time to know who I was and was intent in shoehorning me into a makeshift blueprint.

Twenty years on lithium was being suggested – the numbing of my senses and castration of my vitality under the guise of preventing another psychotic relapse; I was highly suspicious and I thought it was more of an effort to make me compliant and have my behaviour controlled and supervised.

8

David and I have been given permission to visit the games room in a less secure wing of the hospital and meet some of the patients there. Many of us have been associated with Whitchurch for years and have become institutionalised, unable to function in the outside world. Neglect is written onto our faces: many of us have sunken eyes or constantly dilated pupils, twitching mouths (signs of tardive dyskinesia), spasmodic smiles or just blank faces – irreparable side effects of the drugs and invasive procedures administered here. Nonetheless, there is a generosity of spirit between us. We care for each other like a bitch suckling her pups. We have an awkward understanding that life is suffering. Some of us bear physical scars on our bodies – the badges of self-harm and failed attempts to commit suicide. Nearly all of us believe we have had direct contact with God – some of us think we are Him. We mostly subordinate ourselves to other people, ceding authority and responsibility to the psychiatrists and to those who make us believe that they can plan and make our lives better. Many of us believe our lives are at the mercy of a brutal fate dictated by astrological phenomena. Sometimes we proclaim our sovereignty as free men and women in the world, but then we become labelled as having delusions of grandeur. The fact is, we are disenfranchised and possess rights only to a rudimentary life.

This is an asylum full of people being God. We have understood literally the knowledge that there is no difference between the Creator and his Creation; no separation between God and ourselves. It is the most honest place I have ever been in. Extreme fear and fearlessness blend together to create a precarious atmosphere of vulnerability, joy and also chronic sadness, because though we recognise each other as complete, we are broken and alone in our solitude.

*

Becky was a good example. She had a history of being sectioned. Whenever she was free outside, she liked to return to watch her friends and other patients immersed in their games, like ping-pong, or Scrabble. Some sat and knitted, some talked, others just watched the TV or, like her, sat lost in in their own thoughts. It was just a way of passing time. Sometimes, she was moved to extemporise her inner drama by suddenly declaring 'Father, forgive my sins!' She would break out talking aloud to herself, enacting an old emotional drama that should have died in the recesses of her memory but still had the power to burn and eat away at her.

Becky had a disconsolate life. Sometimes, she prostituted herself to make ends meet for her child and herself. She was trapped inside a downward spiral of self-loathing. Far from showing understanding, the community of so-called 'normal' people treated her contemptuously, branding her with sickness while completely overlooking the truth that their own immune systems were too weak to confront the illness that subsists within us all.

*

I saw this African-Caribbean man, sitting upright at a table for hours staring ahead without blinking. He was pretending to write on an invisible typewriter, his fingers tapping incessantly on the wooden surface. I could see he wasn't mad, only that he was completely absorbed in his unspoken unwritten narrative that was somehow mentally alive. Something extraordinary was occurring in his mindscape, and I thought I could read these words on his face:

Look at me with eyes that are gentle, not with a Medusa's look. I'm not a hole in your being, sucking your life away. I am not an unfeeling thing nor are you. My soul whispers like an icy brook melting with the onset of spring: 'I am human'. Words have lost their seriousness. Language is a hollow reed through which a cold wind blows – it makes sublime music but it hasn't helped you in understanding my experience. When we come face to face with each other, our distinct realities disturb each other. We are afraid of each other because our instinct is to murder. Look at me. I am Lazarus. I am the burnt body, the smoke issuing from the chimneys of the death camps... I am the stench and blood that cannot be washed away... We did this to each other.

*

Weeks then months passed and I became more estranged from my body – it had become a thing which I just pushed around. I heard nothing from Anarkali. I tried calling her a number of times. Mostly she hung up. When she did talk, her voice was callous: 'I feel all my dreams have been broken since I trusted you. Falling in love didn't drive you to the madhouse. It was your unresolved issues and egoism. I don't want you. I'm going back to normal, doing my job, being with friends whose company I enjoy. I don't need you.'

Her anger made it the most meaningful thing she had said to me lately.

I couldn't be a hero for her nor could I ask her to rescue me from the darkness in which I had imprisoned myself. I was agitated. I didn't know who I was – because I was of no use or value to anyone despite my loving them. I was not the prize worth Anarkali's rebellion against her father. She had become hardened by his neglect and, to an extent, she was enjoying the sport of reducing me to yet another man needing to deposit his oats inside her.

David and I were in E53 playing table tennis when Janet came in to tell me that a young woman had come to visit me and was waiting in the courtyard. I hurried to the garden in anticipation of embracing Anarkali.

She sat waiting beneath the majestic cedar tree that had been planted decades ago by the mother of a patient who'd suffered shell shock in the trenches of Passchendaele in the Great War. A bluesy autumn breeze blew and there were the shadows of clouds passing across the lawn. It was afternoon just before lunch. The air was mixed with the smell of food being prepared in the kitchen and leaves being burnt somewhere in the grounds. I brushed my lips on her cheek. She bowed her head to deflect any intimacy. The bouquet of her hair filled me with a sense of loss. 'How are you?' she asked, in a matter-of-fact way trying to conceal any emotion.

'Well,' I said, 'the staff here are wonderfully kind. I spend my days hanging out with my friend David. How are you?'

'The usual. My boss is a bitch. She couldn't understand why I had to come and see you.'

'I'm sorry,' I said.

'For what?'

'For putting you through this misery.'

'Oh that. Forget it. I'm having a great time. I'm back to doing my clay sculpting and partying at weekends. I wanted to check if you were alright and ready to get on with your life.' I felt a pain in my stomach when she said this. She had come to say goodbye – to face up to her own feelings of love and crush them, because being in E53 meant I was insane and there was no future with me. It was asking too much from her to show me kindness.

Sometime later, I regretted that I didn't become openly angry. 'Go to hell,' I might have said. 'I understand how to take care of myself. It's the rest of you and your kind who have forgotten how to cherish what is pure. You deny yourselves and make a virtue of your starvation. Love is my bread and wine.'

No such words passed between us and I remained attached, unable to let go of my false image of her.

I walked over to the borders of the courtyard and picked a daisy. She put it in the buttonhole of a faded denim jacket she wore and then I noticed that her eyes looked different, shallow and opaque. Noticing my distraction, she said, 'They're my blue eyes, I treated myself to a new pair of contact lenses.' She paused, 'A friend is taking me to Greece next week to relax. She says the men out there are hung like donkeys.' Then she laughed. I pictured her having sex with other men and tortured myself with the unfathomable despair over her abandoning me forever.

Anarkali was fascinated by my naivety but we were in collision. Though punished by its harshness, she still identified with a world where love was laughable and insufficient – whereas I stood proclaiming it to be the only true ground worth preserving.

There was shepherd's pie, peas, chips, and a glass of orange juice beside my place at the table. David was not eating. He had been waiting. His worried expression faded and his face lit up when he saw me reenter the ward. I took my seat opposite and looked at him. I burst out crying because I realised I wanted to let Anarkali go and sink into the past without ever condemning her. However, with every mouthful of food that I took and wherever I looked, my thoughts were fixated on her alone. In my mind, she'd transformed into an archetype for all people. When I noticed David's lapis blue eyes and red lips, I could see that they had the same essential transcending beauty as Anarkali's.

I was afraid to be left alone. I was willing to debase myself, exchange my freedom to be possessed and owned by her. I wanted the impossible, since I was willing to exchange my life with any other man she might desire. How strange and powerfully strong was the bitterness with which I didn't want to be me.

Despite the soporific effects of the medication, I still felt attuned to an elusive inner sense of being encircled by the work of the

Divine, calmly composing life, writing the destinies of all souls and painting the world. A robin perched on a window ledge, marvelling at life, was imbued with holiness; fiery leaves waved on trees; the news flickered on the television dramatising hunger and privation; the light of the sun, the cosmic soul of all people, was dispersing across the sky – everything was in dissonant equilibrium because of being touched by the spirit of holiness.

'What are you thinking?' David asked. 'You look so sad.'

'I believe that everything I have seen in this life so far is a lie,' I replied.

9

There was nothing more to wait for in E53. The game was over. Luke, who had graduated in Law and was now practising as a solicitor in Cardiff, came to see me. We sat together. He'd brought me a packet of Sobrani Black Russian cigarettes. 'I thought you'd like these,' Luke said. I opened the packet and put it on the table, and we each took one. I inhaled deeply, revelling in the taste and smell of the rich tobacco.

'You know I only smoke these on my birthdays,' I said.

'I know. You could say this is a kind of new beginning. It's quite nice in here.'

'I'm quite happy.'

'Do you know, Michael, that you're under Section 28 of the Mental Health Act. That means you can't leave voluntarily. Your psychiatrists decide when you are fit and healthy to leave, and that might not be any time soon.'

'But they have no right to keep me here indefinitely.'

'They do have the right. It's in their discretion to release you when they want. You may have to apply to go to a tribunal, which means appearing before a judge and panel to prove you are no danger to yourself and the public.'

'Nobody told me this.'

'They think what happened was very serious and it's a relief to everyone that you've made contact with us again and haven't stayed in starry heaven. Besides, you seem to be enjoying yourself at the moment.' He smiled, pursing his lips.

'I want to leave, Luke. Can you arrange for me to go to a tribunal?'

'Yes, sure. I'll get a colleague of mine who specialises in mental health law to look into this.'

*

The day of the hearing soon arrived and I was dressed in an uncomfortable grey polyester suit that Luke had given me.

I went to David's room to say goodbye. 'Remember be yourself. Just relax,' he said.

'I will. I hope they let me go home,' I said.

'They will. Don't worry,' he said.

'Will you come and visit?' I asked.

'You try stopping me. I love you, Michael,' he said.

'Me too.'

My father and brother Atma met me outside the staff nurses' office. It was nice to see them. We sat and waited in the designated area for Dr Edwards to appear. 'I'm sorry to tell you that the tribunal has been cancelled,' he said.

'What does that mean?' I asked.

'It means that it wasn't thought necessary to put you through the hardship of being interrogated by a panel. The team here thinks you are now well enough to return home. As long as you keep on the medication, you're free to go.'

My brother translated for my father who sighed with relief, then awkwardly took Dr Edwards's hand to thank him.

I slept in the back of the car while my brother drove our father and me the long sombre journey home to Leeds. It was a place I no longer fitted in. The television was constantly on in the living room, and when it wasn't dark, I would lie on the sofa trying desperately to block out the world.

All I did for two months or more was sleep. The drugs made me comatose. My body felt like a heavy parasite attached to me. Images of Anarkali continuously tormented me. The few hours that I was awake, I tirelessly repeated to myself the absurd question 'Does Anarkali still love me?' When there was no satisfactory answer, I disappeared into the dismal terrain of my shadow. I couldn't accept her humiliating rejection. My values concerning the nature of love had been torn down and a strong sense of dereliction hung on me.

The medicines were making me shudder incessantly. Nothing made me smile anymore, my face had been broken. I didn't possess the language to express my distress and unceasing turmoil. Every morning, my father tried to rouse me and get me to go to the restaurant with him. But I couldn't budge. He would find me vacant and disconnected when he came back in the afternoons. He didn't stop trying to inspire me to engage with life. When I failed to respond, he'd give up and fall tenderly asleep next to me until it was time for him to return to the evening shift.

I was so detached from my surroundings that I failed to see my father and mother growing closer together. As always, she cooked, but there was a special reverence in the way she prepared the food and served the chapattis and tended to our needs. She would sit beside us watching my father and I eat, her face expressing concern for both of us. She couldn't bear to see my father and I being driven apart.

My father relied on my mother's unquestioning faith that I would regain my composure.

'I've lost my son. I can hardly remember the boy who laughed, sang, danced, and loved life endlessly. What's become of him?' he said.

'He's very ill, my love,' she said.

'I don't see him getting better. How could he have lost his mind?'

'The very things you love about Michael have led him to where he is now. Though I wouldn't wish it on anyone's child, this is part of a journey, that he has to take.'

'Do you think I am to blame for always trying to dictate the way he should lead his life?'

'Don't be too hard on yourself, my love. You too inadvertently hurt your parents and mine by bringing us here. You loved your freedom when we were young but are too scared to allow Michael to experience his life according to his own conscience. Not a single breath can be taken, fires burn or rivers flow, without the power of God. See what our son is going through as a gift from Him.'

'What kind of god could condemn my son to be so lost and in such dreadful pain?'

'I have no doubt he will recover,' she said. 'The doctors here are hopeless. They understand only the body. They are completely ignorant about a person's soul and sprit. My son needs a cure for his ailment. We need someone who can tell us the cause of his being poorly. I believe he can be healed back home in India.'

The last time I had been to India was as a child, now my parents had begun – out of helplessness – to make preparations to take me home again, half insane, in an effort to cure me.

10

It was hot; my body was soaked in perspiration. I refused to take off my fleece because I couldn't stop trembling. A malicious sun was burning across an unending sky infected by congregations of starlings and kites hoisted by people enjoying the early evening on their roof terraces. We were being driven in a rickety Ambassador approximately 200 miles north from Delhi to the Punjab on a journey that would take more than eight gruelling hours. I was feeling anxious about all the times we stopped and the maimed children and destitute elderly crowded the car begging for something, their expressions warning me about unceasing hardship in this unintelligible place.

I recall the indelible image branded on my mind from the last time I was here. I was littler then. My father held my hand as we precariously crossed Chandni Chowk (the Moonlit Square) in Old Delhi at midnight. The traffic screamed around us in the spot where Guru Tegh Bahadur was beheaded in 1675. Hymns from the Sis Ganj Gurudwara – a golden lotus domed Sikh temple commemorating the site of the guru's martyrdom – were being broadcast on loudspeaker, jostling against the riotous cacophony of those ancient streets. In the middle of this historical chaos was a site that was calm, disturbing, and beautiful. An old man who looked like my grandfather sat cross-legged on the pavement. Draped across his lap was the figure of a limp girl whose spine was deformed. She looked as if she was dying and he held out a wooden begging bowl above her belly saying nothing. The old man's eyes were stern without remorse, complaint or fear of his and that girl's fate. Together, they possessed a wondrous aura and the hard reality of a rock found amongst furrows of ploughed earth. People stopped to drop some meagre coins, most just continued on their way. I was deeply ashamed of myself – for what I saw and being part of an indifferent pitiful humanity.

My cousin Narinder, a big red-faced cheerful man, hurried back to the car from a music stall at one of the dusty roadside stops. He had a cassette of songs by Mukesh from whose effeminate tremolo voice he knew my father and I derived simple pleasure. The first song reverberated with me; it was an annoyingly jolly tune counterbalanced with lyrics about a man anxious to see his beloved:

> Night and day the candle swells
> Still my soul in darkness dwells
> Lord knows where is that friend
> My beloved has brought light into life. [3]

I watched people and animals moving through the misty night – I was travelling farther away from the madness of the hospital into an environment that is a riot of exuberant surviving. Having crossed the congested Grand Trunk Road that snakes from the Delhi into the Punjab, we eventually arrived at dawn at my father's verdant village in the north called Amargarh. My parents hoped that being in their spiritual home would help heal my soul.

The car stopped outside the family shrine and as was customary, both my parents lit a small ritual fire in devotional thanks for a safe homecoming. I was made to cover my head with an white cotton scarf and distribute sweetmeats amongst the villagers gathered around; then our neighbours gave us the keys and we entered our house with an inner courtyard paved with marble that my father had built on the site of his father's ramshackle cattle barn. We had arrived with no plans. My parents could see no way except to take me to see the most learned man they knew, a friend of my father's for over fifty years.

One of my aunts heated some water on a spluttering gas stove for me to bathe. After breakfast and greeting other relatives and villagers who came around to the house, my father took out the Atlas bicycle from the storeroom for me to ride. I had to follow behind him and my cousin Narinder as they rode pillion on a moped to the nearest town called Nawanshahr. The town, founded around the late thirteenth century by an Afghan warlord, is a special place for me, not for its narrow winding lanes and rich mix of temples and mosques but because of the memories I have of the venerable man I was about to meet.

I cycled through a level crossing where scores of children and women were collecting coal that had fallen off the passing steam engines. I followed the moped in front a few hundred yards down Railway Road, until we came to a dimly lit, open-fronted dispensary of Ayurvedic medicine. Ved Hari Krishen was a tall sinewy man in his early seventies. With his hooked nose, delicate wrinkled skin, and peculiar sounding voice, he looked like a wizened old crow. He was instructing two women sat on a wooden bench on how to take the powdered herbs that his assistant had just ground.

My father and I entered the cramped shop while Narinder waited outside. My father respected Ved Ji too much as an older friend to embrace him, but deep affection was expressed as they greeted each other. We sat down and waited until his business with the women had finished. A young boy brought some tea. There was a tranquil atmosphere in the shop. Soon my father came round to telling his old friend how sick I was and how he hoped he could cure me.

My treatment with Ved Ji began on the very first day when he looked into my eyes and declared, 'You are between two worlds. You are neither here nor there. This is a state of madness and you will recover.' He read my astrological chart and ordered me to stop taking the medicines. I was to follow his prescription to the letter; there was, he reassured me nothing to worry about, as he would bear all the consequences for me. I felt a sense of inner relief. I instinctively knew he had penetrated my soul and observed my malady. My Karma was in need of repair. He asked me to feed the fishes in the river every Tuesday and on Wednesdays, I was to leave a kilo of rice wrapped in purple silk as an offering at the old temple dedicated to the god Shiva. I asked him to tell me what he saw in my birth chart. Ved Ji replied that once I had made a full recovery he would let me know. In the meantime, I was to make pilgrimages by myself to all the holy sites dotted around my village and the town.

The withdrawal effects of the haloperidol were a torture. I did not sleep for six weeks. At one point quite early on, I begged Ved Ji to give me just a herbal drug to overcome my insomnia. He refused, saying that he was and would be with me through the whole 'trial' as he called it. Soon, I became accustomed to wandering alone along the uneven roads and in the fields looking at painted totemic stones, thinking about the forgotten ancestors whose spiritual presence they marked. I visited small shrines dedicated to deities no one knew and the deserted stone mosque, abandoned after the catastrophe of Partition.

My mother made me wheat balls to give to the fishes and on Wednesdays I prostrated myself – feeling somewhat self-conscious – before the centuries old lingam, a tall black stone in the shape of a phallus symbolising Shiva the Destroyer of Time. I allowed myself to enter into the mystery of the beginning, death, and recreation of the universe. The fear residing in my body began subsiding and a subtle strength re-emerged. The presence of a world outside and beyond the confinement of my narrow conceptual enclosure began to appear. Months passed in this way. The tremors in my body faded and I began wearing my Indian shirt and baggy trousers as I cycled around my village and to Ved Ji's shop every day.

My father's and mother's hopes began to be restored. One evening, my Uncle Saroop remarked, 'The light of your eyes has returned.' I looked at my reflection in the mirror; miraculously, I felt an emotional connection with myself that I feared had been severed forever. I could see my life returning to me. I wanted to relate to the world: the rising and setting of the sun across the plains; the slender poplar trees lining the single-track roads; the rich fields with harvests of sugar cane, potatoes, and mustard leaves; green orchards waiting to fruit. I so much wished to be drenched in life and for my body to be able to withstand its overwhelming power. Once more, I felt the beauty of people getting on with their daily lives: women milking cows in the morning, children dressed in uniforms off to school, the carpenter fixing a cart wheel in his front yard, farmers overseeing labourers in the fields, and the noise of the distant town waking up to a day steeped in frenetic activity.

In India, there is an abiding belief in the complex relationship between life past and present. It was in the land which contained my entire ancestral heritage that I sensed the incorporeality of the boundaries between what has occurred and what is happening today – past and present seemed interchangeable, mirroring and conditioning one another. The future is something radically different to humankind – it is in itself the country in which the sacred holds dominion and from where it approaches us as if in a dream.

As the residual side effects of the psychiatric medicines vanished, it began dawning on me that it is not until we nurture our innate capacity to decipher the metaphorical world that we can truly remember who we are and apprehend reality for what it is. Millions of Indians look upon the Himalayas as being the abode of the gods or as the locks of Shiva's hair while so many of us moderns see these mountains only as an impressive geological rock formation, revealing the evolution of the earth. This world dissolves without the force of humanity's imagination. Who are richer in understanding the work of life? To suspend judgement and believe a child can be born walking from his mother's womb as is said about the Buddha; or to believe that meditating on the Immaculate Conception is to reach out for deeper truths about being alive? Being alive doesn't simply consist of material facts and data. It is up to us in our entire being to discern and celebrate the immutable inner truths that provide our lives with meaning.

I made a full recovery. I had not taken any medicines for over three months and there was no sign of a relapse. I was becoming accustomed to being present in my body. I was happy once more to be alive. The time had come to sadly leave India.

As he promised, the revered Ved Ji read my astrological birth chart. It was a straightforward affair. I was anxious to know if I would have another breakdown. He said that no one was able to predict the future, but that he thought I would lead a charmed life. Then he sighed and said something simple and enigmatic: 'Wisdom is not everything. There is nothing quite like happiness.'

11

I returned to England in the spring of 1993 more humble for being alive and sane. I began working on a Youth Training Scheme as a reporter for a little-known magazine called *Vibes*. I had a wide remit, which was to write up on the arts and news important to multicultural Britain. I was thankful for the gift of working, especially since only a year before I'd been condemned to having no life, let alone a future. Moreover, I found my work endlessly fascinating. The editor left me to my own devices and it was up to me to define my own area of work. I was surprised to find myself writing pieces not only about Bhangra and the Asian Underground, but also about the deep crisis of identity amongst people from the host majority communities – savaged by the uncivilised excesses of Thatcherism and Conservative Party rule. My work got noticed and without ever planning or dreaming it, I ended up on an apprenticeship at the British Broadcasting Corporation as a researcher. Even so, I was melancholic with not being able to share my good fortune with anyone. Many people looked at me wide-eyed when they knew I worked for the BBC, but their superficial admiration meant nothing to me.

Every evening after work, without fail, when I returned to my small flat, I would rake over my affair with Anarkali who I last saw in the grounds of the mental hospital. Even though she'd heard about my wellbeing and good fortune, nothing I could do could impress her. I was stricken with self-contempt and fury at being a nobody for her. In my free time, I'd go down to Tiger Bay and sit on the quayside. I would listen to the sound of ropes clinking in the wind against the boat masts and flagpoles and watch the tide roll in across the mud flats, making the seagulls and warblers rise in flight. I couldn't abide living here anymore – the whole city was soaked in Anarkali's presence and I couldn't stop feeling the pain of never being with her again. I began keeping distant from Khalid, since I couldn't stop myself from thinking incessantly about Anarkali. I felt lonely in his company. Even though he was still caring, I thought I was boring him. To this day, though we promised each other we would, Khalid and I have never really sat down and talked about that tiring testing time when he was my companion and kept me safe during my first psychotic breakdown.

In 1995, after waiting for her for more than two years, I decided to leave Cardiff without finding any resolution. A position had become available in the documentaries department of Radio 4. I applied never expecting anything. I was however duly invited to attend an interview. I was quizzed by a panel of distinguished documentary makers and a woman from human resources who took herself too seriously. I performed well and they were impressed by my work and ideas. It was all a bit of whirlwind. I received a phone call after three weeks offering me the job; I nearly fell of my chair with excitement. The dour HR woman asked if I would accept the job. My heart was racing but I calmly replied that I was very grateful and accepted. The next thing I knew, I had moved to London.

I lived in a compact cluttered but comfortable studio in Goodge Place, a few minutes pleasant walk from Broadcasting House. I'd wake up after intoxicating nights spent in Soho, have coffee and smoke in the kitchen going over in my mind the events of the night before: the bars I visited, the women and men, young and old flirting, the encounters with strangers who became instant friends, the lonely moments spent on benches around the squares enjoying the spectacle of people loving each other and the frivolity.

It was a sad and exciting time. The analogue age which had defined the twentieth century and where I naturally belonged was meeting its demise. The internet and the age of digital broadcasting was being ushered in without any reflection. In sound editing, instead of cutting tape where I listened for the warmth and vibration of people's voices and imagined I could feel the words slipping through my fingers as I handled the material, I was now editing colour streams on computers. Along with many others, I couldn't help but think that something of the imperfections that characterise humanity were being filtered away with the new cold hygienic technology that didn't tolerate white noise and stripped life of its quiet aura. I remember it was 1995 when the internet was rolled out for the most of the staff at the BBC. As a researcher at the time, I couldn't have guessed the devastating effect it would have on the libraries and downgrade the way in which knowledge was acquired, processed, and valued.

I spent the next ten years completely free of manic episodes, making programmes into which I poured myself. I associated with people who thought they were influential. I was perceived as a threshold, a mediator between those who were meant to be decision takers and opinion formers and the wider public. I didn't care about the kudos which middle-class people attached to Radio 4. I was still seeking the approbation of my parents and the immigrants of that generation, who worked in factories and lived passionately for their families. These were my people from whom I felt alienated. They possessed immense charisma, their lives were poetic and made an indelible imprint on my being. The BBC was of little relevance to them and I was angry at the level of ineptitude and ignorance with which that institution depicted the people I loved. There was however one exceptional event where the BBC was forced to accommodate for a few days some of society's disillusioned and marginalised people.

On Sunday 31st August 1997, Britain was forced to begin showing the world a more humane and tolerant side, despite muted protest in parts of the traditional establishment. What happened was a tragic nightmare ending to what the media had constantly tried to portray as a fairy tale. Diana Princess of Wales, her lover Dodi Fayed, and their driver Henri Paul had been killed in a car crash in Paris in the early hours.

I had been unaware of the news having spent all that day secluded at a friend's house, enjoying the late summer weather getting drunk. I walked into the BBC Broadcasting House on the Monday morning a little later than usual, oblivious of the atmosphere and went straight up to the fifth floor where I worked in documentaries. As I walked down the grey-carpeted corridor, I noticed several yellow Post-Its stuck on doors asking me to go see Anne, the head of the unit who was looking for me. I checked my watch and saw that I was only fifteen minutes late. Nevertheless, I began feeling nervous, thinking that perhaps I was going to get sacked. I went to Anne's office who got up immediately looking anxious as she called me in.

'You've heard about Diana?' she said.

I must have looked incredibly stupid because I didn't know who she was talking about.

'Diana, the Princess of Wales, died in a car crash last night. You've been asked to join the special events team that will do the outside radio broadcast of the funeral.'

'When's the funeral?' I said, slowly beginning to understand the seriousness of what she was saying.

'We don't know yet. The Royal Family are at Balmoral Castle and there have been no palace announcements so far. Go meet who you're working with and read all the papers. You need to get up to speed fast.'

I genuinely felt it at the time to be a privilege to be working with people who showed immense professionalism. My job was to find and talk to the 'ordinary' people who had met Princess Diana and whose lives she had touched. We were going to record their memories and these 'vignettes', as I called them, were to be edited on tape and played as intervals to 'add colour' during the live broadcast of the funeral.

I worked endlessly, sleeping very little, building up a portrait of a woman whose innocent dreams had been crushed in a marriage that fell apart. Slowly, as the week progressed, until now unseen numbers of Black and Asian people, those with disabilities, those brutalised by landmines, homeless young people, and many queer people walked through the grand art deco entrance of the BBC to give their accounts of what an astonishing woman she had been. No one I recorded showed any signs of hysteria or hyperbole. What I witnessed was often a calm, sometimes tearful but dignified telling of the touching compassion shown by the Princess. I was moved by the powerful impression she'd made on these people as they talked with a beautiful emotional articulacy that put the BBC pundits to shame.

It was a punishing week of work. The night before the funeral it had poured down with rain. The producers went for a walk around St James's Palace where Diana's body was resting. They came back overwhelmed by the scent of the mountain of flowers that had emerged in tribute to her, unsure about their own feelings. Incomprehension was on their faces; they didn't know who was in control. Many of the executives who thought they understood how the media worked had a real sense in this instance that it was playing catch-up with the public mood. The Royal Family had come back to London earlier in the day and the Queen made a dignified broadcast to the nation, softening criticism of her blind adherence to outmoded protocol. The sense of crisis that had been building up had abated, and things appeared to be returning to normal, to the relief of many editors who felt that their deference to tradition could again be restated. The Princess had been a maverick. She hadn't played by the rules. What rankled many people was the sincerity in her kindness and the charitable causes she championed. She didn't fit the shallow celebrity cult of the tabloids which was easier to praise, control and demolish.

I was up before dawn on the day of the funeral which was to be broadcast to radio listeners around the world from the Radio 5 Sports studio in Broadcasting House. James Naughtie was presenting the programme. He had written a wonderful script and described the scenes as they unfolded along the funeral procession like a remote seer watching the television monitors. Over the course of the last few days, my colleagues and I had produced about thirty packages to be played. In the end, only a few of them were used. The solemnity of the scenes in London had taken over. I remember the young princes walking behind the coffin, and the crowded interior of Westminster Abbey. I felt my sympathy rise for the Princess's mother and Dodi's father who looked grief-stricken and confused. I watched and listened to Earl Spenser's electric eulogy in the studio, where everyone was stunned. Unable to bear it any longer, I left the studio, went to my office and got my portable Roberts radio. I walked through the empty Arts Unit onto the roof terrace where I could see London spreading out southwards down Portland Place towards Westminster Abbey where hundreds of thousands of people had gathered. I was alone except for a few seagulls squawking wondering where all the traffic had gone. I rolled a cigarette and put on the radio. As I smoked, I listened to John Taverner's 'Song for Athene,' penetrating my body that was aching with exhaustion. For the first time, I felt united with a nation. Then I burst out crying. No matter how much I wanted to belong, I sort of knew that I would always be part of that constituency of the rejected and downtrodden since I too now felt that I had lost a friend.

1 2

Work monopolised life. I often worked late into the night. I loved watching the sunsets from my office window to music that I blasted from the stereo system after everyone had left. I ate in the BBC canteen; sometimes when I happened to finish early, I shopped at Tesco's on Goodge Street and cooked a late meal which I had in my small kitchen. I have a notion that my colleagues liked me though they believed that I could be too serious and lacked the nonchalance and wit typical of many of them who were educated at public schools and Oxbridge. I didn't care much for what they thought. I committed myself wholly to the delightful painstaking work of trying to sculpt in sound radio features that caught the essence of people's lives: what they did, thought, and aspired to. Deep down I was lonely; I yearned for camaraderie. It was unusual for me to be invited out by BBC people for a drink much less a party; I don't think I was being excluded – in hindsight, perhaps I was being taught a rather crude lesson in knowing my place which attenuated my lifelong conditioned feeling of being tolerated but never accepted. It could also have been that people sensed I was a rather private person. I did, after all, hide the fact of my past mental illness and concealed my unhealed pain of Anarkali's brutal rejection, which I still felt five years on.

*

I met Sevim on a Sunday during the languid summer of 1998, when London pavements had flowered with stylishly-dressed people eating al fresco or standing carousing beneath city lights and dimly seen stars late into the evenings. I had nothing to do and decided to go watch a poignant Russian film by Alexander Sukorov called *Mother and Son* which explored the relationship between a dying mother and her son in an isolated ethereal landscape. Wearing my oversized navy-blue Burberry long coat (a gift from a friend), I walked through Bloomsbury to the Renoir Cinema, a small modernist venue in the Brunswick Centre which was a fifteen-minute walk from where I lived. I'd arrived early, so I stood in the foyer smoking. She was working as an usherette and was serving drinks and popcorn behind the bar. I noticed her short cut hair, thick set eyebrows, slim shoulders. She wore a silk and cotton jacquard shirt and brown Farrah trousers. She possessed an indefinable beauty; femininity blended with an androgynous boyish quality. There was a delicate care and enjoyment with which she served her customers. I could sense that she was interested in me and I wondered if she was drawn by my oddity. I decided to buy a coffee. I observed her as she filled the cardboard cup and stirred in the milk and sugar. 'Where are you from?' I asked.

'I'm Kurdish from Turkey,' she said. 'And you?'

'I'm Indian but I was born here.' I said. 'What religion are you?'

'I'm Alevi. And you?'

'I'm Sikh.'

'Shouldn't you have a turban?' she asked.

'I suppose so but I carry my faith in my heart.' I replied.

This was turning out to be a real conversation. It had felt like an oblivion since someone had been interested in wanting to connect with me. Most of my relationships had become superficial. Sevim was offering me warm-hearted friendship, which I really wanted.

'Which caste do you belong to?' she asked.

I was surprised. No one who wasn't Asian had ever chosen before to explore and place me in the context of caste.

'Sikhs aren't meant to believe in caste,' I said. 'But since you ask, I am Kashyap Rajput. My ancestors brought water to the cities and we were also known for being brave soldiers. What about you? What is being Alevi?'

'That's a difficult question. Alevis follow an esoteric Sufi path in Islam. We revere being human. Heaven and hell are created by our actions in this life, and God is present in the here and now in all living beings and nature. Our task is to nurture our higher qualities and compassionately serve the good of all humanity,' she said.

I was touched by the authenticity of what Sevim said. I asked and she gave me her telephone number. I followed up a few days later and we became good friends. It became our habit to meet outside the cinema usually after the last show. I would leave work late as usual and often not arrive on time. Then we used to meander along the side streets of Clerkenwell listening to each other talk about our lives. Sometimes we stopped off at Exmouth Market to drink and smoke together. We loved and respected each other. I valued our platonic friendship, especially since Sevim's sincerity was an antidote to the hard work routine and superficial relations I'd become accustomed to. Ours was literally a pedagogical relationship. We walked for miles every evening just sharing whatever was important in the moment.

She was a film student at the London College of Printing. Our conversations were hardly ever about the cinema which she loved – the films of Tarkovsky and Parajanov's *The Colour of Pomegranates* being her all-time favourites. Instead, we engaged in spiritual matters, the meaning of religions (which we both found interesting) and what we were doing with our lives. I was safe enough in Sevim's company to confide everything in her and she in me.

'I don't think your relationship with your boyfriend is going to last,' I once said out of concern after what she'd told me.

She shrugged and said, 'Everything must end sometime. It's just how we bear the pain that matters.'

She held herself with immense poise. She listened carefully when I told her of my turmoil over Anarkali and she made me laugh by observing simply, 'Well, she was wasn't very polite, was she?' About my psychosis, I saw that she understood. She was genuinely interested in what happened to me as an alternative experience of one's psyche, though she wouldn't wish it on anyone.

Many months passed this way. Spending time with Sevim had begun to heal my heart. I frequently attended the vibrant gatherings at her brother Murat's house with whom she lived. It was a commonwealth of nations: friends who were migrants, refugees or visitors just passing through London on their way to somewhere else congregated here.

We entertained ourselves by singing folk songs or reciting poems, be they in Turkish, Kurdish, Farsi, Arabic, Hindi or English. Candles lit our soirees and the large living room of Murat's house would be crammed full of people wanting to dance, perform or talk and spend some precious time together in a city where communities are constantly being splintered and broken. Everyone cooked and brought exotic dishes to eat like mecmek kofte, Persian pilaf, foul mademas or lamb curry. Those times were a feast for the senses. There was the profusion of tastes and colours of the food, the delicate scent of flowers adorning the room mixed with the perfumes the women wore, and the absolute value we attributed to life in our celebrations. I felt at home. Here I too was made to look upon my own beauty even though I was shy to admit it.

Sevim's and my friendship was profound. We felt we would continue our companionship forever in this manner. It wasn't at all inevitable that we should become lovers.

It happened one morning after we had been to an all-night party. We'd left around 4am. The sky was a canvas of inky twilight just before the sun had risen and the air was thick with birdsong.

'Let's walk,' Sevim said.

'Where to? We've already walked,' I said.

'Let's go back to your house.'

It must have taken us over an hour from Kentish Town to Goodge Place getting lost along the back streets. The sun had risen by the time we arrived back at my flat. We had a little breakfast of toasted bread with strawberry jam and butter with coffee. I put on an early morning raga by Pandit Bhimsen Joshi, whose voice shimmered like the febrile quiet before a storm.

Josh, my brother-in-law, was the first one in my family to hear about Sevim. He was delighted I had found someone who understood and cared for me. He thought Sevim was beautiful when he met her. 'She looks like a woman in an old Mughal painting,' he said. 'Your sister won't be pleased she's Muslim. But then again I'm not pleasing to her either.'

Fortified by Josh's response, I decided to introduce Sevim to my mother. She and Sevim embraced each other lovingly. My mother beamed. I was inwardly moved as I had been nervous about what she was going to think. My fears were allayed. They were two extraordinary women who instinctually recognised each other's strengths and weaknesses. 'You are very kind, my child. You shouldn't work too hard,' she said as Sevim massaged her feet and arthritic legs with her healing hands. The question of our being of different religions didn't even occur to my mother who saw the human being in everyone. 'There is no Hindu nor Muslim. We all come from one source, which is the light of one God,' she said. When Sevim told her about her Sufi background, my mother was excited; she'd become convinced that she must be the girl from a noble family that I was destined to marry as prophesied in my birth chart. It was something I hadn't considered.

PART 3

1

It was a sunless winter's day in 2003; drizzle dripped from a grey sky. We woke up around 6am to prepare food and tea to take along on the march and wait for friends to appear. It had been a long night of drinking, smoking grass, and arguing the rights and wrongs of going to war against Iraq.

My colleagues at the BBC had been in a state of excited commotion over the sensational claims made by Downing Street that Iraq's Weapons of Mass Destruction could hit London within forty-five minutes. All the newspapers, radio, and TV were replete with stories of the imminent chemical and nuclear danger posed by Saddam Hussain's venal regime. The pale-looking Prime Minister, who believed he was on a personal mission from God, had, with the exception of a few principled objectors, unanimous support from Parliament to take the country into war. He mocked the pacifists and those who opposed the war, calling them appeasers, skilfully spinning out his speeches, sentences usually embellished with three synonyms to give them a rhetorical gravitas. I felt smothered every time he did this. Even when I allowed myself the thought that this war could at least be justified, his grandiloquence made my defence weaker in front of friends who weren't journalists but were nevertheless more attuned to the subtle nuances of the truth and could decipher them very well in the tone of a speaker's voice.

The Prime Minister's loquaciousness was a malignant force betraying any real concern for the thousands who would be killed by our bombardments. Neither did he care for those he thought he was saving. Again and again, Saddam had shown a "flagrant, brazen, undisguised" abuse of human rights. I make it up as I write, but the effects of the Prime Minister's exhortations and tortured facial expressions were nauseating. Instead of considered, critical persuasion, he seemed intent on bludgeoning people into submission of his will. He lacked humility.

Sanctions had already destroyed Iraqi society. The corrupt Oil for Food Programme had done nothing to lessen the immiseration of millions of people. In return for billions of dollars' worth of oil, we were shipping food to the Iraqis which was unfit for human consumption along with basic medicines past their due date. Hundreds, possibly thousands, of children, the elderly, and the vulnerable had died and were being killed by easily curable illnesses like diarrhoea, because there were no medicines. Baghdad's morgues were full, shops shut, pavements lined with people selling what little possessions they had and even their precious books. The Prime Minister and his sharp-suited cohorts ignored the human tragedy of Iraq. They failed to inform the British public of the facts of human suffering caused directly by our actions. In their unprincipled amorality, these politicians demonstrated neither remorse nor kindness and as such failed in what ought to be the first duty of the offices they held: to care for those they represent. There wasn't even going to be the pretence of appearing to listen to the world.

I stood in the garden of Milton Grove in Stoke Newington, smoking in my boxer shorts, the wind dancing in the branches of the trees. A cheap, moth-eaten cotton blanket that I had bought in Varanasi was draped around my shoulders. I was feeling warm, humble and protected against the cold. I imagined I looked a little like Mahatma Gandhi in a simple threadbare cloth. Ever since my childhood, photographs of Gandhi had captivated me. With his bespectacled gaze, Mahatma's entire life appeared to be absorbed in that single moment of a camera's click. I nurtured a passionate attachment to his ideals of simple living and love conquering hatred. From the kitchen, I could hear Guru Nanak's soulful song for God, whose name he said was Truth, streaming from the radio.

Sevim was preparing breakfast. Her hair was tied back and her bangles jangled rhythmically as she rolled out the dough for parathas. Cooking didn't come naturally to her and she was clumsy in the kitchen. Her cheek and forehead were smudged with flour and I smiled, remembering the men and women with ornate painted marks on their foreheads, praying on the banks of the Ganges as candles burnt in the indigo twilight before dawn.

Sevim always thought about how much her food would nourish and be enjoyed by our friends, even though she was overly critical of herself. I wanted to whisper in her ear, perhaps because it had been a long time since I had said anything gentle to her. I missed her very much. I wanted to reassure her, 'It will be alright. I'm not to blame. Please forgive me.' At moments like this, free from monotony and argument, whenever I had time to reflect, disenchantment gave way to a little space of serenity. Anguish against which my world was being quietly eroded, for the time being, at least was subdued.

*

The time when I had been sectioned had receded in my memory. For ten years, I had worked creatively in a demanding position without being on any medication. I didn't even so much as take an aspirin. Much of what Ved Hari Krishen, had said in India had turned out to be correct. It seemed true that the psychotic episode I'd experienced was due to the intensity of emotions that flowed from a true falling in love. My madness had seemed to correlate with the Eastern understanding of it being a heightened or alternative state of consciousness that needed to be integrated in the psyche. There are many love affairs recorded in Indian literature where at least one of the lovers becomes mad with passion. I felt my experience in Whitchurch Hospital all those years ago had been similar to that of Majnun who became insane after losing his beloved Laila. Now after a decade, I was finding it difficult to do 'normal'. Perhaps I was missing the adventure of the seemingly never-ending high. I'd become disillusioned.

I longed to hold Sevim's hand and walk naked through woods beside a river. She would lay her head on my shoulders and rest easily. But I was now distant from the first spontaneity that had attracted us.

Like flowers drowning in too much water, an excess of sublime sentiments had overwhelmed me and over the interim years, I had lapsed into mundane dailiness. Nothing heard or said held much meaning for me now. The silences between Sevim and me were becoming longer and saddening for her. Sometimes, without any reason, she looked at me with eyes clogged by inner grief. I felt angry and guilty at the same time. My conceited belief that she was playing the victim compelled me to hurt her even more. There were just so many insignificant words floating through the air between us.

Life had lost its vivid aura, because, without ever intending to, I had turned away from the person I loved – mostly because of the residual dross of the brutal rejections in my life. I could not comprehend why Sevim alone continued to think the world of me. And so this war and the protests against it were just other perfunctory events amongst many – they didn't really matter at all to me.

The rain stopped. The inky sky dissolved into a polluted dull grey, accentuating the silhouettes of skeletal branches and sleeping tower blocks and dreaming rows of chimneystacks on top of black-pitched roofs. A bone chilling wind blew across the city.

Gulsum (Sevim's sister) was the first to come down: thick tangled white hair, flecked with strands of black, fell down the sides of her strongly defined face. She lit a Marlborough looking thoughtful. She had been vociferous last night about the ugliness of war. Gulsum was naturally loud and passionate because she tended to believe that no one listened to her, even though what she had to say was important. She possessed an indomitable will. Outwardly, she never admitted the possibility of being wrong and took dissenting opinions as a personal attack and sign of disloyalty. Gulsum believed my adherence to BBC rules of impartiality as dishonest fence-sitting and insipid.

'For God's sake, who are you, Michael? Where are you?' she had said the night before. 'Why do you want to see me anyway? You try to censor the way I feel and express myself. I am angry for the young men who are dying in Afghanistan. Boys who haven't even had a chance to live being sent to their death, forced to leave their mothers and fathers, wives, and children because of lies and greed. What is this?'

Incomprehension, a stubborn refusal to be indifferent to human suffering was Gulsum's power. She never overcame her grief over her father's decision to leave the remote mountain village she loved and migrate to Istanbul in the early 1970s. She became a foreigner in her own country at the age of thirteen and a tyrannical surrogate mother to all her siblings, including Sevim who was the youngest in a family of eight.

An open fire blazed in the snug living room adjoining the kitchen and it was not long until it was full of a babel of beautiful people. There was Calen, an old Etonian, celibate homosexual, and scion

115

of the Irish landed gentry. He was unable to form any lasting attachments having never overcome the heartache of being sent to boarding school when he was only seven by his parents who he remembered as always fishing in the rain and entertaining the literati. After Oxford, Calen had taken to hanging out in the poor areas of Dalston and Green Lanes with Turkish men, seeking the companionship he sorely wanted. He had an endearing charm. I recollect him as being unassuming and diffident yet possessing a sharp supercilious wit against politicians and their vulgar solutions. His best friend, Leyla, stood beside the fireplace protecting him. It was apt that she was a therapist since her name 'Leyla' denoted the darkest part of the night in balance with the moon. She was a voyager into the unconscious labyrinths of the mind. I felt close to her, but also sensed that her immense compassion had waned over the years. Her intensive training meant that it had become part of her nature to analyse everyone she met. It was sad for me to realise that Leyla had begun to disbelieve in the tears she often spontaneously cried for her fellow human beings. Then there was my cousin, Meena, an intensely engaged woman, a social worker afflicted by the ills of society, the brutality that families and individuals inflicted on each other. Meena was constantly torn between her ideal of there being a core human goodness and the degradations she witnessed on a daily basis. She had found her anchor in her husband, Eamonn, an intelligent and humane man who sat on the worn Soho sofa tending to their two-year-old daughter called Maya, a source of unending joy.

We tramped down the quiet street clothed in warm coats, hats, and scarves. A number of houses were displaying posters denouncing the impending war: "Not in My Name", "Don't Attack Iraq", "Bring our troops back", "Bliar"... Newington Green looked bleak. Two centuries earlier, this hallowed place had been a haven for anarchists and dissenters like William Godwin and his wife, Mary Wollstonecraft. From here, they launched their blistering critiques of the leviathan state that denigrated and imprisoned humanity. They raised their glorious voices in vindication of the inalienable rights of women and men the world over. The spirit of the French Revolution had penetrated their bloodstream and their religion was *Liberté, Egalité*, and *Fraternité*. What would we be shouting in the Westminster wilderness? What message did we want to convey to a callous government? Although no one knew what to expect on that February morning, I felt that this was an appropriate site from where to begin a solemn lonely pilgrimage.

*

The Routemaster number 73 brimmed with excitement as it transported its passengers to University College London. Thousands of restive people were corralled in Gower Street waiting to be set free like a conference of birds on the march to Hyde Park. I picked up a yellow placard of Tony Blair wearing a teacup on his head and holding an automatic weapon: "Make Tea Not War" was the slogan. I was happy to march under this insignia since it highlighted the absurdity of his posturing. I wanted to satirise and ridicule him personally and the banners in rainbow colours proclaiming "Peace" made no sense in a world manufactured to be careless. I wanted to believe that I was wrong this time. My blood thumped through my body as the clamour grew and soared like a host of organs lifting their hymn up to God. Despite my deep isolationism and unwillingness to ally myself with any one party, I was enjoying what became a confluence of hundreds of thousands of people lending their voices, their feet, their entire being to each other. We were the people, this was the middle ground, the chimerical chalice of politicians, spin doctors and their minions made flesh. I was looking into myself as was everyone else I marched alongside. It was an astounding conversation where one word was being uttered by millions in unemotional London and across the turning world and it was 'No!' A painful scream, a slave's dignified refusal to comply with a master's command, a commotion calling simply for peace.

This anti-war march affirmed what the great philosopher Heraclitus of Ephesus thought over two and a half thousand years ago. He said, 'That which is in opposition is in concert, and from things that differ comes the most beautiful harmony.' [4] This is a perfect description of the protests which took place on 15th February 2003. People of every class, creed, and religion speaking a multitude of languages came together to create a harmony that felt more beautiful than anything I had seen or felt before. Through Mayfair and Piccadilly, right up to Hyde Park, an immeasurable river of individuals was in unstoppable flow, but beneath the plethora of banners and colours, we were united in one single body. It would have cured Heraclitus' despondency. He had observed despairingly, 'It is not possible to step into the same river twice'. For him, transience of life was everything, rendering knowledge impossible. Today, at least for a moment, Time had been arrested. Although the war was inexorable, the call for peace echoed unceasingly everywhere. We were repeatedly bathing in a fountain of moral certitude that had somehow emerged in the world, challenging the global elite and their makeshift order.

*

Eamonn carried Maya aloft on his shoulders. I sang to her Leadbelly's rasping rendition of 'Down By the Riverside' with its gorgeous refrain "ain't gonna study war no more". My companions and I all stopped for a break near the Royal Academy. Spirals of steam swirled out of our cups as we drank the sweet Indian masala tea and helped ourselves to Sevim's aloo parathas.

Gonna meet my mother down by the riverside,
Down by the riverside, down by the riverside
Gonna meet my mother down by the riverside
And study war no more. [5]

Gulsum was amusing Shahan, Leyla's little boy. Calen joined me in singing. And all of us watched, becoming increasingly resigned as the crowd continued to pass without end. I stopped and said to Meena, 'They're not going to listen. This isn't going to achieve anything.'

'It shows,' she said. 'There is no such thing as the public good. They're making out this war is about bringing democracy to Iraq. Well, until now, Saddam Hussain was our son of a bitch. America and Britain made him. We supplied him with the chemical weapons in the war against Iran, which he subsequently used in the killing of the Kurds in Halabja. Those massacres were collateral damage – the actions of a friend, the cost of maintaining regional stability in the interests of American foreign policy. This war is nothing but a greedy stampede for oil.'

'But why now?' I asked.

'Because they have the power and they can,' she said.

'Do you really think Britain can sign up to an illegal war without a second UN resolution?' I asked with feigned incredulity.

'The law is there to protect and justify American violence. It's a foregone conclusion. Blair is Bush's window dresser. He's the poodle. He's the person presenting the front that etiquette and international protocol are being adhered to. His arguments keep changing and it reveals his desperation to begin this war. There's enormous pressure on Hans Blix to produce a smoking gun. I tell you that man has incredible integrity and I'd be surprised if they don't try and discredit him.'

We rejoined the throngs of people marching. My happiness waned. I felt grief at the thought that once more I belonged with those inflicted with torment, the subjugated, and the defeated. There seemed to be no end to the supremacy of the powerful. They have won and turned to their advantage nearly every historical battle. The past is strewn with promises broken by the elite and the blood of the slain. My mind began straying and wandering over the past. I saw my father, who had died nine years ago, marching alongside me, his arm strung about my shoulders. And there was my grandmother who had not even heard of my being born, standing with her hands folded together in salutation. Beside her, there were hundreds of other souls I did not know. I was intimately connected with all the people I was seeing. They had died in obscurity but their dreams, yearnings, and prayers for a benign and just world were vibrantly alive. They were praying to be redeemed in the present. There is no happiness without redemption; there can be no redemption until we have listened to the previous generations silenced by death and oppression. Happiness is after all the secret of the concealed soul. We must create a world today that takes into account the wishes of the deceased as well as of the generations to come.

We eventually entered Hyde Park. The cold seeped into my bones. I was shivering all over. We stood far away from the stage and could barely hear the speeches. I could already hear the bombardment of Baghdad creeping unnoticed across the green. I was sorrowful and confused. 'Meena,' I said. 'I wish my father was here with me.'

'That would've been nice,' she said. Then she smiled and added, 'But we're not alone. Big Brother is here watching us.'

PART FOUR

1

The story is everything. In the digital age, every person is merely a means to an end. I don't like it, but I have been forced to accustom myself to tossing people aside just after they've broadcast their most intimate thoughts and feelings. There is no room in my life for anyone else. A pseudo-professionalism prevents me from striking up a more humane relationship with those who I interview – a shake of the hand seems sufficient. My emotions are interred beneath the demands of an inflated ego. I am feeling the pressure mount and am on the edge of bursting. My heart is aching to be free. I am resentful of the mean time constraints and efficiencies imposed by self-serving managers. I look around me in the BBC and can only think of a few good people who are still thoughtful and caring about what millions of others get to read, see, and hear. The mediocre self-serving majority who lack ethics are only intent on climbing further up the food chain, kicking those below them all the way.

I was sick of this fucking game and wanted out, but I was just too scared to let go. I had just bought a house in an enclave in Stoke Newington in London where all the streets are named after famous poets which I like: Shakespeare, Milton, Shelley, Byron... Sevim didn't want it and was disturbed by my impetuosity. 'Don't worry,' I told her. 'We can afford it. I have two shops as part of my father's legacy. Why should we postpone our lives for tomorrow when we should be living today?'

It was a beautiful tall Victorian house with four bedrooms, polished oak parquet flooring, and inglenook fireplaces. It was a place where I imagined spending Christmases just like in the books and movies, where perhaps Sevim and I could start a family. I was elated when we moved in but the interest alone on the mortgage, which was over £2000 per month, felt like a noose around my neck.

*

'Dog bites man, no story. Man bites dog. Story.'

So goes the adage amongst newsmen. But we've reported in this manner for decades now. Constantly seeking out the abhorrent that adheres in the world is making me ill. There is no time for reflection, critique or compassion to grow. Perhaps I'm not any good at what I do, since nearly everything I produce and inform the public about is incomplete. While I don't doubt the virtues of scepticism and of suspending judgement, what about those important moments of lucidity where one clearly knows what is ethical, just, and true? Must I, even in these instances, appear to be neutral? I don't, for example, see the balance in simply reporting Africa as a heart of darkness, abounding with starvation, civil strife and corruption, not without making bare the unspeakable legacy of racism, slavery, colonial rape, and slaughter which we in Europe and the US perpetrated.

So much prejudice and falsehood is pedalled under the guise of impartiality and quite often, a pseudo-truth is manufactured that is one-sided, reflecting only the interests of the powerful. I remember being in the lift with Henry Kissinger, escorting him out of Broadcasting House after he walked out of a live studio where Jeremy Paxman had tried grilling him over his role in the illegal bombing of Cambodia. Kissinger, who looked decrepit despite his expensive suit and shoes, was in a foul mood. I recall how terrible he smelt. Perhaps it was the stench of his anger with Paxman, or the death of hundreds of thousands on his conscience. 'Have you read my memoirs?' he asked.

'Some of them,' I said.

'I wrote every word with my own hand,' he said.

You're such a terrible, arrogant man, I thought.

I can't even pretend to know the truth anymore. I am dismayed by having to repeatedly give space to well-paid, eloquent speakers fielded by powerful factions whose job is to dazzle and render the opposition impotent. Facts are important but they never speak for themselves. It's the way they are presented and who is spinning them that determine their meaning and relevance. When Christ said that he had come to 'Testify to the Truth', Pontius Pilate asked him, 'What is truth?' I imagine silence to have been Christ's response. This silence was the ground upon which Christ stood, his fearless compassion for his fellow human beings, the poor, sick, and dispossessed. The Truth is always profoundly ethical; something can't be true if it is immoral. 'Don't kill love' – is the maxim at the heart of Christ's stunning silence. It humbles me and fills me with wondrous trepidation.

Recently, I was talking to an intern. I asked her, 'Why do you want to work at the BBC?'

She earnestly replied, 'I want to change the world and make a difference.'

I didn't know whether to admire her or laugh at her vanity. Working at the BBC had spoilt my idealism. Like the preacher professes, I felt I was striving after wind and there was nothing new to be gained under the sun. I was weary. I'd been thrashing around for a kind of salvation from this shallow circus. I wanted to do something meaningful with my life, rekindle a space for myself in the world, and abandon this spiritless intellectualism.

2

The house that Sevim and I bought in Milton Grove had a racing-green door. I had hung a small frightening mask with wide black eyes and red tongue on the front door, so as to ward off people entering with bad intentions. It was an open house. It felt right that many people were free to visit us and stay over. It would have been filthy and uncharitable if we kept our privileges to ourselves.

The house was always full. Gulsum often came round. Everything I know which is of value has been learnt by accident. One such life lesson arrived on a very ordinary day. Gulsum, Sevim, and I were sat at the back of the long kitchen around an old zinc-top table beside the French doors that opened on to the enclosed walled garden. We had our cups of tea and smoked. There was a feeling of harmony between us, and whatever emerged from it was meaningful. I listened to them talking about being Kurdish and how their culture was filled with hardship and unceasing sadness. I observed Gulsum becoming mournful and Sevim looking reflective. I was surprised and touched when Gulsum wiped her eyes and said, 'I like England. I feel more relaxed here. People here have manners. They know how to keep a proper distance. They detach themselves. Not like us. We become over involved in other peoples' pain. It gives meaning to our life. We cannot exist without pain. English people are more enlightened than us.' I had never thought of the English stiff upper lip as a virtue. It was probably the first time that I felt enriched and thankful for being born in England.

The journey taken by my wife and her family was completely different from my own. Sevim was only two years old when they migrated from the middle of Turkey westwards to Istanbul. But Gulsum had already drunk deeply from the wellspring of a people constantly under threat of physical and cultural extermination. She understood very well the suffering of her community. Her father's songs about freedom, separation between friends and lovers and their reunion, the poetry of an aching soul healing the sorrows of people who led difficult embattled lives embedded themselves in her body. She had learnt to take on the distress of other people, even when they themselves were unaware about why they were hurting.

People love Gulsum. To them she resembles a healing, totemic figure from ancient times, exuding an enigmatic presence. Gulsum's affection has no boundaries. The tragedy is that her loyalty carries high expectations. It is conditional on other people being aware and revealing their true nature, which is seldom possible. Social waifs and strays gather around her because she soothes their shame and whatever they find objectionable about themselves, but this makes her existentially tired.

3

The night is blissful. We are stoned. We are lying down in different corners of the room. Sevim is reclining elegantly on her side like a statue of a sleeping Buddha. Gulsum, like a protective lion, has spread herself out near the entrance. I am prostrate on my front, floating on a galaxy of stars. After about half an hour of submitting myself, I stand up and look through the window. It is raining. There is a powdery drizzle making the yellow rays of the streetlights look fuzzy. The light from the white headlamps of cars speeding by is reflected on the road, and for once I am oblivious of the traffic noise, which is normally a constant irritant in our house. My attention falls on a puddle on the opposite side of the road, beside the footpath, beside the care home for drug addicts, alcoholics and society's maladjusted who seem to like Sevim and me and look out for us. I focus in on the ripples made by someone splashing through the puddle. The waves ripple to-and-fro across the surface of the water measuring time like a metronome, upsetting the stillness before the beginning of a thought, creating a disturbance, but then always graduating towards restoring equilibrium.

'What is fear?' Sevim asked. She was curious and wondering aloud. It was like an invitation to a sermon.

'Fear is a refusal to seek oneself,' I said. 'It is a refusal to see the Self as being completely immersed in the universe. Fear prevents Man from accepting that his destiny is with God who is ultimately within himself.' A feeling of awe rushed through my body. The puddle was resonating with meaning. I looked around myself. The whole room, the dirty polluted sky above, the wooden floor on which I stood, the wet dual carriageway, the concreted front yards, the slated pitched roofs covering hundreds of miles of this city – everywhere was suffused with the spirit of holiness.

Sevim began singing softly in a melancholic minor key, a Turkish song about the journey of a human being from the womb to the grave. All of a sudden, I began to feel that I could no longer sustain my own weight, as if something leaden had landed on my shoulders. My legs began shaking underneath me. I tried resisting the overpowering force, then acquiescing, I knelt down and folded my hands in prayer.

I was talking silently to myself inside the room, wonderstruck by a spiritual instant transcending comprehension. A police car was passing. Its siren pierced the midnight calm. Gulsum woke up. Her face was bathed in light. 'What was that?' she said.

'A police car,' I said.

She looked at me bemused. 'Michael, are you alright?'

'I'm praying,' I said.

She lay down again, laughing raucously. 'You're stoned,' she said.

4

The only time I managed to be authentic, to relax the disguises I wore, was away from work. A sense of despairing disintegration had taken hold and was beginning to gnaw at me. I felt deeply discontented with life. I never thought the experience that led to my being in E53 would ever recur. My vigilance had over the years been replaced by lassitude. In hindsight, it was natural that I would break down again. My existence was blown asunder not long after the aerial bombing of Iraq had begun. The ignition for my ensuing madness was not a falling in love this time, but an anguish in my stomach about the meaninglessness of life, the mindlessness of the world and its inexorable march towards death.

Sevim stood in the doorway of Milton Grove early morning.
'I love you, darling,' she said.
'Me too,' I said.
'I'll miss you. Look after yourself. Keep well.'
'I will. We'll have fun when you're back.'
'Don't work too hard.'
'Don't worry.'

The sun was resplendent that morning. I was on my way to Broadcasting House feeling lonely. Clouds were moving from afar through a placid blue sky towards me. Sevim was at home. She was preparing to go to Turkey later that evening. I had felt her anxiety and it had stayed with me. She was probably doing a hundred and one things right now – cleaning the kitchen, ironing, calling friends, and paying bills – treading water as always, trying just to keep afloat, keep breathing. I felt subtly emotional (I light a cigarette as I am writing – and take a deep drag. Perhaps the feelings are more intense than I want to remember). I was sort of tearful. I was carrying inside me a sense of hopelessness. Something had remained silent between us and I felt torn away from her.

I have never been able to reconcile myself with the realisation that parting and loss are woven into the tissue of life. So much of my past had crumbled and its rubble preserved inside my body as a dim memory. The hospital where I was born had been turned into a block of flats, the schools I attended in Leeds demolished or turned into supermarkets, even E53 had ceased to exist. I dread irretrievable loss.

As I walked embalmed in the golden hue thrown over the city, I was aware only of the pavements supporting the mass of concrete, brick and mortar towering above the ground. I crossed over University Street and ambled past UCL Hospital and the people revolving around the accident and emergency unit. Then I thought I heard a vaguely familiar voice say, 'Everything is infinitely divisible.'

It had been over a decade since I had been in interned so very sick in E53, but in this ephemeral instant I was thrown back there. Something removed from the natural world was announcing itself again. I could hear, inside the timbre of this voice, a passionate longing to reunite with me. I was touched by the simplicity of the statement.

'Is everything divisible?' I asked. I listened for the response.

'Yes, everything. Nothing has a material substance. This world and your existence, you and your consciousness originate out of Nothing.'

I was unprepared. I felt myself becoming anxious. My breathing became erratic. I began trembling as I became suddenly aware of my own absence. I was experiencing this world and everything in it as a canvas of appearances beyond words and thoughts. There was no comprehensible essence to existence. As people, we are only dust and reflections of everything around us. I could find no meaning, reason or moral order to life. Whatever I believed was joyful flooded out of my being like notes of a symphony played off a page – the music delights only once but then is lost forever. I stood there alone feeling a constellation of emotions like remorse; bitterness, envy, and anger that shone and fell like stars above a desert. I tried to remember who I was but was no longer able recall the steps I had taken on the journey from my birth to the present moment. All my history had been erased, I didn't know who I was or what I was doing here. My ego had been punctured. It had ceased to exist. It had only been a collection of impressions enabling me to function, but they bore a scant resemblance with reality.

Every day is different; every day, the grass changes, is refreshed and renewed, but for the Ego, all things remain identical and always the same. Now that I could clearly see my ego was an illusion, it along with the world around me seemed to disappear and cease to exist. The surrounding environment felt uncanny. I was so detached from myself that I became fearful even of my own heartbeats syncopating the continuance of passing time. I couldn't remember being born, living, and growing up. Who made me? Where did I come from? Why? An unending flood of questions like these sounded like the complaints of a sick dying man.

I wasn't going to make it to work. The entire street with its furniture of signs, cars, people and buildings; the smells and changing play of light and shadow became a vertiginous labyrinth where I had lost all sense of orientation. I shook under the rolling thunder of unexpected inner desolation. I sat down. It brought about a momentary relief and realisation that I was at a crossroads, trying to maintain my memory or surrendering completely to the onslaught of forgetfulness. Simply surviving was not a choice. I sensed I had to let go altogether the life that I had known. My praying was in vain. I recognised that this terrible situation was without ending, because my frenzied instinct to preserve myself would not accept defeat. I tried saying, 'I am something,' but it came out as 'I am everything'. These words became silent screams reverberating around my seemingly unfathomable and empty being. How could I not refer to myself? I was beyond care and understanding. I was trapped inside a solipsism. There was no escape from the fields of infinite nothingness that the strange voice had cut open inside me.

An old woman of about eighty with a stooped back curling over a well-worn walking stick limped down University Street. She stopped, scrutinised me carefully. There was curiosity in her bright eyes. 'Are you alright, love?' she asked. I felt her sense my distress. She beckoned me with her hand to come sit beside her on a nearby bench. 'Are you in trouble, son?' I shook my head, not knowing what to say and took out my pouch of tobacco and began rolling a cigarette. 'May I also have one?' she asked. I gave her the one I had made and rolled myself another. We sat smoking silently listening to the world around us. I felt uneasy knowing it to be a strange situation. Eventually, she said, 'Where are you from?'

'I'm not sure,' I said. 'I'm Indian but I was born in England.'

She smiled and said, 'None of us really know where or what England is. But I lived in India once with my late husband. He was stationed in Simla. It was a beautiful place up in the mountains. The people were very nice, very welcoming towards us. But I do remember that we were quite unkind towards them. It was quite understandable when they wanted us to quit their country. It was the right thing to do.'

Her name was Marianne. She was a lovely creature with the fragrance of freshly cut flowers and I wished she would gather me up into her lap and lull me to sleep. She was completely serene and solemn in her body. Her silken complexion was like parchment. It spoke of a life lived full of integrity and honest feeling. She wasn't at all afraid of me. Rather, she respected me and showed concern, as she would have done to her own son. And I felt close to this stranger as if she had been my own mother.

I wanted to tell Marianne about my dad and how much I cried when he died almost a decade earlier on a trip back to India, soon after I had begun working at the BBC. I was granted compassionate leave and I flew out to India. At first, I couldn't express my feelings. Crowds of people flocked from surrounding areas, to his village, to give their condolences. I heard the women spontaneously burst out in heart-touching keening, beating themselves as if a great hero had fallen in battle. I sat alone listening to the women's walling, which formed a dramatic soundtrack for the older men to recount my father's life and deeds. The man who was being mourned and talked about seemed alien to me. It was only back in England, when at last I found some time to be alone in the woods behind my house, that I began sobbing inconsolably. I hugged a tree trying to impede the onslaught of tears. I was angry that he should have chosen to escape after being gravely ill to India to die, without being near me. Leaving me behind was a betrayal of sorts.

I looked at Marianne, trying to understand what we were doing together. I was filled with bewilderment and could not resist the impression that at that moment she and I were actually presiding over his funeral. I was seeing the subtle fire of his cremation dancing seductively upon his purpling corpse. Then in a remarkable moment of synchronicity, Marianne turned to me and said, 'You can't fill your father's shoes. It's finished for

Man. The ages where God was apprehended by Man and where He presented Himself to us are long over. Anyone who thinks of themselves as a prophet or professes to know God is a little nuts.'

I felt compelled to acknowledge her and, without inhibition, I knelt down and kissed the ground before her. Marianne got up and walked away unperturbed. A small memento, a song of redemption from the Upanishads that could so easily and probably was written by Pete Townsend, surfaced in my mind: 'Brahman is everything. It is silence, it is nothing and yet it is you.'

As I sat on my island in the middle of University Street, a calm understanding began to dawn on me, that Nothing exists before God and yet it comes from Him and suffuses everything. Only Nothing, the Unground in its entirety is whole – it's not subject to time or space, death, and rebirth. On an ordinary, nondescript day I had been suddenly stripped of my persona and laid bare to the unending nature of my heart. A fire had been lit inside my body and all my senses given up to the universe as an offering. My eyes opened with wonderment and closed with tiredness and reopened to discover that the world had changed. My body was being refashioned out of a ruin. A refreshing wind blew through the street, creating a little dust bowl, turning the litter, making the treetops bend. A weight seemed lifted from my shoulders and my heart skipped. A puppy padded along, a young woman tried holding down her skirt, a traffic warden was doing his rounds, cars continued fizzing restlessly to wherever they were heading. The scene was a balm for my mind and eased the tension around my head. I lifted myself up and began walking towards home.

5

The war raged on in Iraq even after the Western Alliance had declared victory. Hundreds of people were still being killed. In some towns torn down by battles, many bodies were left to rot in the debris, to be consumed by wild dogs and flies in the broiling heat. Relatives and friends mourned their loved ones. Iraq had become a country of grieving neighbourhoods. At night, army patrols supported by gunships continued their assault. Their mission was to assist the government, protect civilians and disarm terrorist militias. It was a travesty for the innocent civilian population. Women and children were amongst the casualties of the invading army's technological superiority and victims of the brutality of whoever we called "terrorists" or "insurgents". Hatred and desire for revenge were implanted in the hearts of many who survived. The roots of this tree of bitterness sank deep into the earth. The forsaken young inherited their grandparents' dream of freedom and justice. Many whose homes were destroyed or relatives killed withdrew into bewildered grief. Others were driven by rage to fight. During the day suicide bombers attacked in crowded places, destroying generations of lives in acts of indescribable horror. Improvised roadside bombs were being used to slaughter young men from the occupying forces. I couldn't – as a human being – carry on living a "normal" life, however remote the upheaval and violence appeared to be.

I was too sick to be nursed at home. Sevim was in a dilemma. She was reluctant to have me sectioned.

'What's happening, Michael?' Sevim asked.

'It's Karmalila,' I said.

'What's that?' she said. 'I'm sorry I don't understand.'

I too was lost as to what I meant. I couldn't concentrate. My mind was in flood. After a long pause, I replied: 'Well, it's the play of God.' More silence. The arms of the digital clock moved methodically without any sound. 'We are all toys, puppets in the games that the creator likes to play,' I said.

'Do you know how it's making you feel?' she asked.

I didn't. Everything outside and inside me was abundantly sentient. I felt touched by objects, people, words, and thoughts. My heart bled. I felt an immense heaviness as if a rock was lodged in the middle of my chest. I was abandoning everyone who loved me, because of a pain I felt unable to endure. Sevim looked emotional. I realised that I was not making myself understood to her. And it was a deep torture to explain what I was experiencing. 'Michael. Twelve years ago, you had a psychotic breakdown. It might be happening again. Do you understand what I mean?' she asked.

That was when I had been dissected by love. Now all I sensed was the pity of life. I could hear the lament of someone crescendo in my body. It was the grief of someone ashamed of his passivity in life watching the planet disintegrate. The pain also stemmed from my mother's agony and guilt when she gave birth to me. The environment here was totally alien. In India, birth betokened a gift from God, in Britain one sensed a feeling of it being sinful. When I appeared, she couldn't hold me. Her refusal to comfort my distress alarmed everyone not least me even though 'I' was not yet fully formed. One can say that solitariness was my first nourishment and lesson in life.

I looked dismayed at the parquet floor that I had waxed painstakingly, noticing the scratches that I'd missed. The walls that Sevim and I had painted buttercup yellow felt as if they were tombstones. Even though no one apart from Sevim and me were in the room, I felt a crowd of people sitting around the empty table beside the window, with its kitsch orange floral plastic table cover. I sighed. There was a book of paintings by Marc Cagall on the table. A dreamlike depiction of Chagall cradling his wife Bella as they float above the snow-clad Russian town where they were born resonated with me because of its absolute faith in magic. My half-finished copy of it with its naïve lines and colours lay beside the book. I looked at Sevim with her clear eyes. 'I think I should go to hospital,' I said.

'No. Perhaps there are other better ways. Would you like to see a psychiatrist who Leyla has recommended? He's very experienced and could possibly help you get through this period.'

'Okay.'

'Would you like to take some medicine before seeing him or can you wait?'

'I prefer to wait. But what do you think?'

'As a temporary fix maybe we should take you to the GP and get something. Is that alright?'

'That's fine.'

*

Sevim arranged an appointment for me to see Peter the psychiatrist in Harley Street. It was an immaculate cold day with towering cloud formations moving through a bright lapis sky. Sevim held my hand in the cab. It had been many days since I had stepped out into the open air and stared nervously at the world passing on its noisy way.

There was a large vase of lilies producing a pungent fragrance in the grand entrance of Peter's opulent Georgian building. We were asked to wait in an adjoining room until he was ready to see me. Impeccably dressed in a Savile Row suit and Oxford brogues, Peter walked down the spiralling staircase. This Englishman immediately impressed me. I thought he possessed the manners to charm angels. The gentleness of his voice and natural empathy made it seem like he was communicating directly with my soul.

He invited me into his room and offered for Sevim to join us for the first session. I sat opposite him in a comfortable chair doused in bright sunlight. Sevim placed herself on the periphery of the large room. At a time when I believed I understood all things but knew nothing and was fascinated by what seemed to be the profundity of my thoughts, Peter asked me a simple sobering question: 'Can you tell me what "too many cooks spoil the broth" means?'

I fumbled and realised that I didn't know the answer. Mentally I could write a treatise on proverbs and their meaning. But this was not what Peter wanted. He was looking to create a safe space of transparent mutual respect where one is heard without prejudice. It was humbling in the gentlest way – the first moment I knew that I needed help to cure my predicament.

I sat in his comforting presence investing my faith in him. Peter recognised what he described to me as 'Rapid Cycling', which referred to the intense connectivity and congestion of my thoughts, moving from one thread to another without any real completion or development. He diagnosed me as having a bipolar affective disorder.

'Would you like to work with me?' he asked.

'I would like that very much,' I said.

'But I have some quite strict conditions. You would have to see me every week for at least the next six weeks. It is expensive but we could make a financial agreement. What do you think?' he said.

I looked apprehensively at Sevim.

'Your health is more important than anything. We shouldn't worry about money. We'll find a way,' she said.

When Sevim and I left his room, I felt as if I had brought Peter with me. I came to regard him as a friendly voice and compassionate man. The conversation that had been sown flowered in my mind. Whenever my thoughts needed direction or I sought an impartial voice, I mentally summoned the image of Peter, enthroned in his consulting room to guide me.

*

I began spending my days walking in circuits around Clissold Park with my woollen hat pulled right down over my ears, thinking about my failures and meditating on God. Very few leaves were left on the trees. The paths I took were often damp and muddy. Except for the coots and moorhens floating on the water and then scuttling onto the grass, the ponds were sullen grey. When the sun was setting, I would make my way back home. Sevim and I would have a simple meal. The conversation was sparse. I felt at peace with my melancholia, though at times she appeared troubled and grief-stricken. It was selfish of me to have turned inwards. I couldn't express the personal and paradoxical joy I felt except by being solitary. When Sevim went to bed, I would begin talking with myself for hours. I became totally absorbed in playing different roles of people I loved and despised.

One quiet evening past midnight, I tidied the cluttered living room. I caringly brushed the handwoven rug made in Anatolia, which spoke to me of the troubled story of that war-torn region.

When I was ready, I summoned Peter into my imagination, to begin my ritual play. 'I hope you don't mind being called to my humble home at this inconsiderate hour,' I said.

'Not at all. It's always a pleasure to see you, Michael. How can I help?' Peter said.

'You are kind. First, please make yourself comfortable,' I said happily guiding him towards the threadbare armchair.

'Are you expecting other people?

'Yes, the Prime Minister's been invited. I've proposed that he and I have a duel.'

Peter looked alarmed. 'I don't want to be party to an assassination,' he said.

'Don't worry,' I chuckled. 'The duel will be a dialogue; a struggle between Blair and me to look each other in the eye and speak only truthfully. You will judge the winner.'

'Oh, that is interesting! I'm already excited. I've been quite bored recently. And to be teleported here into Stoke Newington – well it's just marvellous,' said Peter.

I stood in the middle of the room, walking in small circles around the Anatolian rug in my Indian pyjamas, while Peter made himself at home. I was uttering prayers under my breath. Eventually, the figure of Tony Blair materialised, dressed in upper-class evening wear and looking a bit over-tanned.

'Welcome, Prime Minister,' I said.

'Yes, thank you,' he replied, looking surprised. 'I was expecting an audience.'

'I'm sorry, I'm not the Pope. I am just a simple man who wishes to speak with you. And this is Peter, my psychiatrist.'

'How do you do, Prime Minister, very pleased to meet you,' Peter said, rising from his chair with his hand outstretched.

'This is highly irregular. I left a party of some extremely influential people to be transported here. Who are you?' Blair said.

Peter sensed his unease. 'Please, Prime Minister, take a seat. I'm Peter Sunsir, a consultant psychiatrist and this is my patient, Michael Nangla, who's undergoing a psychotic relapse. Let me explain. We're both here because of Michael. He has the ability to communicate so lucidly with his own mind that he can make anyone he talks to appear before him instantaneously. We are figments of his imagination. If Michael can get the answers he's seeking, he can be cured of his malady.'

By now, Blair's suntan had disappeared altogether. 'This is astonishing. I will of course try and help,' he said.

'Brother Anthony, I'm very upset about the carnage you caused in Afghanistan and Iraq,' I said.

'It was completely unavoidable...' Blair replied, putting me off with his contempt and boredom.

'Brother...'

'Please call me Tony.'

'It wasn't inevitable, Brother Anthony. It should never have happened,' I continued, trying to the control the game. 'You killed thousands of people, displaced thousands more, and caused devastation across an entire region. The repercussions are being felt by millions and the trauma will continue for generations to come. This discussion is very important. We must both only speak the Truth. Anyone caught lying will either cease to exist altogether or be sent to the nuthouse and the key thrown away.'

At this point, Peter noticed that Blair was trembling with fear. 'Prime Minister, rest assured you won't actually die. What Michael means is that you could have a nervous breakdown if you fail to tell the truth. The worst that can happen is that you may be sectioned or treated at Downing Street with atypical psychotropic medication,'

'Prime Minister, do you agree?' I asked.

'Yes, of course. I have nothing to hide,' he replied, hiding everything.

I went into the kitchen and brought back three mugs of tea. Blair was beginning to feel a little more comfortable. Peter was in raptures.

'This is very civilised,' he said.

'Isn't it?' I said.

'Thank you, Michael,' Blair said, not meaning it at all.

The tea was having the same effect as wine. Eventually, I stood up in the middle of the room and began.

'You said your actions over Iraq would be judged by God. Well, I'm afraid this is the best you're going to get. What was your intention in taking the country into war with Iraq?' I asked.

The Prime Minister looked more relaxed. He was an expert on this well-rehearsed subject, even though this was an unusual supernatural situation.

'My intellect told me that Saddam Hussain had to be eliminated,' he began. 'My personal intention was never to grab oil – although for many others in authority this was a profitable consideration and positive side-effect of war. No! For me, it was simply an issue of conscience. I knew that a brute like Saddam could never be trusted and would eventually prove toothless against the real threat in the region which is Iran. I couldn't stomach the mullahs in Iran calling the shots in the Gulf. What you must understand is that the world had radically changed after 9/11. We were no longer indomitable. Our citizens were at risk in their own homes. The enemy had to be stopped. The enemy is that part of the world that envies our wealth and supremacy.' Blair was looking quite vexed and had begun punching the air as he spoke. 'It was incumbent upon me as a leader of the civilised Western World to kill the spirit of those that envy our wealth and supremacy and dare challenge our way of life. I was absolutely determined to put Radical Islam back in the box.'

'So do you fancy yourself as a sort of prophet?' Peter asked.

'I am not sure I would put it that way. But I do have the intellect to think fifty years ahead,' Blair replied.

'Nevertheless, Iran is stronger now after the damage you did in Iraq,' Peter said.

'Well that's because the idea of democracy that most people have in the West is flawed. Democracy doesn't work in countries like Iraq because they are not culturally equipped for it.'

'Do you think Iraqis are primitive?' I asked.

'Well yes, I do. The truth is, we did the Iraqis a disservice by imposing democracy on them. Honestly, we don't really care much for democracy here either. Elections are bought by massive corporate capital in America. And here in Britain, the political class have a real disdain for the electorate. Either Mondeo Man is just concerned with what goes on in his own back yard or is just plain stupid,' he said.

'Prime Minister, I just need to ask because it's not clear to me: why do you dislike Iran so much?' Peter said.

'I am not sure myself. It's just that these Persians have the chutzpah and strength to keep our imperial ambitions at bay. We and the Americans orchestrated the coup that overthrew their elected Prime Minister, Mohammed Mossadegh, because he dared to nationalise our oil. We bankrolled a quisling Shah and his family, spent millions on creating a supportive middle-class. However, their own historical sense prevailed, and even the intelligent middle classes joined in to bring to success the 1979 Revolution and establish an Islamic Republic of the Oppressed. The Persians believed that they had established a state that would raise the downtrodden. That was the bit that stuck in our throats. Not the Islam – after all, some of our closest allies are the Arab states. The fact is the Iranians are idealists claiming to represent the masses – people who in my opinion don't deserve a voice –it's a step too far.'

'Good God!' Peter said. 'You make yourself out to be caring and paternalistic, but you're just a complete bastard, aren't you?'

The Prime Minister smiled. 'Well it's common knowledge that my father was illegitimate. As a consequence, it's probably more accurate to say I'm the son of a complete bastard,' he said, trying to crack a joke.

Peter winced.

I tried maintaining my composure before an increasingly ebullient Prime Minister, but in the end, he simply had to hear the truth.

'Your crying for the soldiers who died in Afghanistan and Iraq is a sham. Concealed within your sentences is an immortal hatred of humanity. Your over-developed rationality is your sickness. Anything resembling love is quashed in your psyche. Your guile has created bloodshed and disequilibrium. You wanted to perform in front of an audience but in this room, before my psychiatrist Peter and me, you have revealed yourself in all your treacherous perfidy. I can see from your face the terrible effort it takes to be you,' I said, my voice brimming with emotion.

Peter was smiling and waving his mug of tea. He was intoxicated with my speech.

'You're not insane. What is your condition?' Blair retorted.

'It is love, Brother Anthony. I'm a friend of those you would diminish and murder with your brutish intellect. We want peace, justice, and equality here and now in this world.'

'No wonder you're mad. How can a smart guy like you believe in all this nonsense? It's just a romantic dream.'

'This situation, this world is just like a dream,' I said.

'Bravo,' Peter shouted, toasting me with a gulp of tea.

'Cleverness will not prevent you from meeting the doom that you have created for yourself. Your shadow no longer frightens me, Brother Anthony. Freedom is the destiny of all humankind and your attempt to reduce human beings to perpetual servitude will not succeed. I refuse to be like you: a virus enmeshed in a web of biological fatalism bringing disease to every environment it inhabits.'

'Those are not my words,' the Prime Minister said.

'No, but they represent your intent nonetheless,' I said. 'Nothing can absolve you from your crimes.'

The Prime Minister looked as if he'd seen a ghost. I turned to Peter: 'What is your judgement?'

Peter pointed at the Prime Minister. 'That man, the one I voted for, has caused unfathomable suffering. In the hearts of millions of people here and around the world, he's already judged as a scoundrel. What would you like to happen to him? How can we punish him?'

'I don't know,' I said. 'Death by irrelevance?'

'I am in pain for having witnessed your encounter with such a conceited and cruel being. You can if you wish have this wicked man imprisoned,' Peter said. He looked around the room. 'Is there anything that can free you of the foulness of this man and bring you some solace?'

It was past 3am. Sevim was stirring in the next room. I felt as if I had achieved nothing. I looked at my collection of spiritual books from all religions and reached out for my pocket edition of the Psalms. I solemnly read out loud the words on the opening page, my voice brimming with hope that the writer's vision might come true and sadness the time for this to happen was still so far away:

> Blessed is the man
> Who walks not in the counsel of the wicked,
> Nor stands in the way of sinners,
> Nor sits in the seat of scoffers;
> But his delight is in the Law of the Lord,
> And on his law he meditates day and night.
> He is like a tree
> Planted by streams of water,
> That yields its fruit in its season,
> And its leaf does not wither.
> In all that he does, he prospers.
> The wicked are not so,
> But are like chaff which the wind drives away.

I was tired. I knelt down exhausted and rolled up the Anatolian rug. I hoisted it onto my shoulder and walked out of the room bidding my guests goodnight.

6

My mind is drifting. I'm sat in Peter's therapy room where I can be, do and say whatever I want without being judged. 'I am scared. I'm constantly crowded out by memories. I can't distinguish the past from the present,' I say.

'It's important to be in the here and now. There is no other reality apart from the present moment,' he says.

'But this moment is an illusion. The present doesn't exist. All we have is the constant foam of ephemerality, carrying with it a multitude of dead souls. I feel so sad that this life is fleeting.'

'That sounds fatalistic. Aren't we free? To be and more importantly to love?'

'Yes, we are free! And yet we have to fulfil our own destinies. I feel estranged from Moses's God who said "I am Who I am". That's an authoritarian voice because it restricts humanity in its time of freedom. How can we continue speaking to such a God who doesn't tell us who he is. It's painful that he doesn't speak to us and answer our questions. I want to see him but I don't even know who I am!'

'Is there anything wrong in saying you are Michael?' Peter asks.

'I'm that and much more. A name is just a convenient appellation that reveals nothing about oneself. My mother was right when she said "Everything is an illusion. The world is

Samsara – a cycle of death and rebirth." All material things are a shadow of an eternal essence that refuses to show itself.'

'But these things you talk about Michael are real – as tangible as you, me or your mother. I suppose even the illusion is real.'

PART FIVE

1

Sevim is observing the plants in the lush garden. She's wondering at the force of nature and the fruits of her hard work during the preceding autumn. I so worship the twilight. A gentle tepid wind is blowing. A few raindrops have begun to fall. I am sat alone in the semi-darkness, listening to a record by Kishori Amonkar, called 'Recreating a Dream'. Her voice weaves desolation and ecstasy into an early morning raga. She is calling on Shiva to awaken, anticipating the end of the crepuscular darkness by the sun's unfolding. Evening and morning are bound together in my listening. It gives me peace. Nothing is out of place. Everything in the room and my surroundings, the houses beyond the window, the balcony garlanded with lilac wisteria, the robust sycamores adorned with white and pink spindles, books and the distracting noise from The Shakespeare pub, all create an unworldly harmony.

We had been consumed by helplessness in the face of life with its burden of difficulties. Sickness, debt, and unwillingness of many of those I loved to help in any meaningful way led us to selling our house. One night, as I lay restless in bed possessed by worries about the possibility of our home being repossessed, Sevim reached out to hold my hand and said, 'I love you.' She was

147

appealing to me to get well. For her my recovery was invaluable, whereas I felt I was worthless and thought there could be no redemption. Yet the selfless ease with which she was close to me spread through my being. For a moment, it felt comfortable being at home locked in her long tapering arms. I despised the unnatural and automatic way I ordered myself to remember the purpose of my being born. But hearing her words in that quiet night becalmed the turbulent feelings of grief buffeting my soul. Perhaps Sevim's love was after all a talisman for my deliverance. It was as if she was rubbing a healing salve on my wounds without provoking the hysteria that had lately become my habitual behaviour. Most of my companions had abandoned me and drawn back into the quotidian of their middle-class existence. I had lost my rationality. I detested myself as a failure in what I perceived was a wasted life. My lack of emotional articulacy was abysmal. I didn't want to go down, but that was the inexorable trajectory of my fate. I was failing to protect the woman who had breathed life into my corpse. I wished she too, like Anarkali, would abandon me.

Let me waste into oblivion.

'I am loved; I am at one with the one I love.'

This is the feeling that Sevim gives me. This kind of balance, formed out of love, can be an ethical basis for taking action in this life. It is the basis of Karma. In Indian thought, Karma literally means action and knowledge of it asks certain questions. Who is the real self behind the mask that acts? Who is it that talks? Who is it that behaves in a particular way? Who is it that sees? This entire universe is a cosmic theatre without end. The sages said that the art of action is to be practised without any attachment to the outcome – this acting or play is everything, since in and through it the Divine realises itself. Acting from unconditional love devoid of egoism is a fundamental law of action. The repeating journey of a life into death and back into life again is contained and happens every single lonely evening in the existence of a human being. In sleep, we retreat into solitary night union with our inherent ancient self. As I type these words, I feel the will that praises the Sun and Moon at the dawn of humanity swell inside me. I yearn to reconnect with those men and women who nurtured such a profound union with the natural world which has sadly atrophied over millennia. Only scant impressions of the wondrous sentiments our ancient ancestors must have felt remain, preserved in texts, rituals and traditions being expunged by catastrophic consumerism. The whole point of the present battlefield is to preserve what is precious to this life – it is in Mahatma Gandhi's loving words to 'become the change you want to see'. My mind and body will inevitably die, but my soul cannot be burnt, drowned or destroyed and will continue until this planet and time have been dashed and all returned to the peace of Brahman.

2

I tried returning to work but felt appalling anxiety. I felt completely immobilised by the ineffectuality of paid labour in easing my problems. Money could not resolve my feeling about the meaninglessness of life. Peter had prescribed lamotrigine, a stabilising drug, "to smooth out the adverse mood swings" I was experiencing every day.

*

I am sat on the comfortable grey couch, looking around Peter's room in Harley Street. I am wet from having coming in from the rain and feeling cold, despite the warmth of the room. It's been many years since I have worked in the media or done any meaningful work and I can't really afford this luxury of seeing a private psychiatrist. I'm living on a meagre existence of a few hundred pounds a month. My brothers have taken most of my father's legacy. For years, I have feeling robbed by my family and bitter at what I saw was exploitation at the BBC.

I desperately want Peter to tell me I'm a wonderful, kind human being. He knows Sevim is distraught at my inability to work. I want him to tell me to get a grip and stop wasting my talent. But he is too compassionate to even think such inconsiderate things.

'How did you feel around the time you left the BBC?' he asks.

'Terrible. I had no money. Words had become meaningless. I felt life at the BBC was just a performance. My colleagues and me were acting in ways and saying things which seemed untruthful, or at least we didn't mean them.'

'Did you feel that you were the only authentic person?'

'No. I was really afraid and depressed. I was constantly worried about whether there would ever be a reprieve from the vast mortgage I had taken on. I despised myself for being susceptible to the capricious vicissitudes of a capitalist system. I felt the system consuming me. It was like an animal grinding my bones, sucking my marrow. You know, the system is a parasite – it reduces human beings to carrion. Its real currency is misery, pain, and violence.'

'What makes you afraid to work?'

I was quiet for a while thinking how to answer.

'Something inside feels violated,' I said. 'Generations of my family worked in low-paid, physically demanding jobs, so their children could have time to enjoy a less gruelling life. But I feel betrayed by the state, government, and people who were meant to protect me. This capitalism appears to me an invidious way of life, deceiving men and women to abnegate their sovereignty and souls in the pursuit of an illusory happiness.'

Peter's look is concentrated. I think there is a smile of recognition. He's acknowledging the truth of what I am saying. So I continue.

'Everything is brought down to the cattle market of buying and fucking others over. I am paranoid and mystified by the power the system has over me. In my mind, it assumes the form of an immeasurable entity with a consciousness composed of the most brutal elements of human desire. The Free Market possesses me. It manifests itself in a God-like fashion: omnipotent and self-sustaining, vengeful and gracious, espousing freedom but totalitarian in its execution. The lifeblood of capitalism flows from a human mind seduced by its own conceited symmetries.

We worship the unnatural market law that human wants are limitless and resources limited. But it seems to me that we are like flowers: too much sunshine and we wilt, too much water and we drown. My madness has taught me that while our desiring is endless, it has a goal – that is to respect and reunite with the love that is within every person. My needs on this journey are actually very little. We have all renounced something precious to be on this earth, yet so many of us find ourselves in deserts of lonely sand where nothing has value except for the price.'

Peter's timekeeping device sounds. 'Our time is approaching an end,' he says. 'Thank you for sharing with me. I know that it is financially and spiritually difficult for you at present. But you are already pulling through your darkest periods. Maybe in time you will reconnect with like-minded people who share your values and care for you.'

I left the therapy room, but the conversation continued in my head. I saw Peter in my mind and silently carried on conversing with him. Being Peter's patient had given me the space to think about my father's death. Perhaps I saw him as a surrogate father, transferring onto him the feelings that remained unresolved in life.

*

The consultant at the hospital called my brothers and me into a private room in the cardiac unit. He said, 'Your father's in a critical condition. He has suffered a severe heart attack and is very weak. I am sorry to say that it is highly improbable that he will be able to leave the hospital alive.' My middle brother began crying. We all sat quietly expecting the doctor to say something more, but we felt our father's time to die had come.

Dad lies in his hospital bed. I am reading Keats beside him. He is listening to some shabads on my Walkman. It's my idea to help him relax, listening to the holy words of our gurus about life's transience and redemption through their loving grace. He is absorbed and looks peaceful. Now and again, I lean over my book and touch his hand in which there is a needle connected to an overhead drip. His skin is soft and wrinkled. He looks at me and smiles. If he could understand the spirit of Keats' words, he would love them. When my father drank with friends, he often liked to recite Urdu poetry:

Faithful one, let me drink inside the mosque
Or show me that place where there is no God...

I believed it was time for him to take stock of his life. He looked sad. He was trying to build enough strength to let go of the responsibilities he felt towards his sons. He'd always looked after them. He'd seen too many families, including his own, destroyed by sibling rivalries which ended up in terrible fights, even fratricide, and extreme never-ending periods of silence. My father was wondering whether he could save his family from such a fate.

Now he felt powerless and was surrendering his soul to the holy songs which he was listening to. I overheard him complaining to Josh: 'Only Michael comes to see me from early morning until night. The others have their families. There is no one to look after him.' My father was surrendering himself to die listening to Sikh scripture, while I read Keats, and yet we were both on the same page, connected by a golden thread that all that ever needs be known is that Truth is Beauty and Beauty is Truth.

3

Sevim works very hard as a teacher. She is worn out by the loving care she gives her children. I try my best to cook and clean before she comes home but I have essentially lost my capacity to do things other than what is basic to my own rhythm. When the rough winter light enters the bedroom and falls on the bed, the feeble rays of a new day fill me with feelings of exhaustion, nausea, and sickness that life should continue. It isn't anything as gross as wanting suicide, but a subtle tremor vibrating through my fractured being. I wish I could erase my inner world, cease to exist, and miraculously rise up as something completely different. This is the deep pain of consciousness: in life there is no real meaning or value other than those we choose and create.

*

One morning, I had a moving dream. My father, a young girl who was about four years old, and I were walking around an ancient town in the East. The buildings were crumbling and no one appeared to live there. The air was infused with the scent of blossom. The little girl was an orphan. She wore a green sweater, her hair was cut short, and her skin was the colour of almonds. Her forehead was adorned with a small black bindi. I was dressed in loose white clothes. The little girl held my hand. She thought of me as an older brother. She loved me because I was taking care of her. When she grows up, she will ask me to marry her.

All three of us were walking tirelessly from house to house in blinding sunshine. We were at peace with one another. My father's face was youthful. He was walking beside me. I felt the arm of his protection and sensed the warmth of his love. He was glad to be with us. We climbed up some steps of a pension. A man opened a set of twin doors to a large room. It was bare. From a balcony, one could see a silvery river meandering through a forest. There were no boats. I gave the man some money and took the room for the little girl. That was it, as far as I was concerned. It was putting aside any responsibility. My father and I left the child alone in the room. When we were outside, my father turned to me. He was smiling and said, 'I didn't mean for you to leave Sevim alone. You should've lived with her.' I looked back and in place of the girl saw an angel looking at me with tears in her eyes.

*

I am alone in the house not wishing to get out of bed. My mind is working through a web of dreams. My father appears again looking serene. The wounds his death inflicted on me never healed. There is deep longing to meet him again and sadness that this will never occur. I see him on the phone trying to talk to me – I observe him, trying to read his lips, but I cannot understand what he is saying. And there is the image so clear in my mind of the last day when we said goodbye.

It's four in the morning, around two hours before sunrise. My father is looking at me holding back tears, his heart swollen with pain and longing. He's dressed in his tweed coat, he's wearing his NHS glasses, he's still unsteady on his feet – it's only been a month since he's been out of hospital despite what the doctors expected. What is there in his soul that he wants to let go of? It's cold – I go to kiss him and then bend to touch his feet. He holds my hands and stops me. 'We'll do this later,' he says. Another car was supposed to be coming to take me to the airport. 'We'll say goodbye later.' We had been so close. He knew that he would not return from India. I look at him, and I have a strong sense that this will be the last time that I see him. I am sending my father to his death. The car leaves, I see it moving slowly into the darkness towards the end of the drive, and then turn right out of sight. He's gone.

I went inside and sat in front of the gas fire. Birdsong rose slowly in the waning darkness as streaks of red began appearing in the eastern sky. Dawn approached. I stared into the fire, seeing in my mind the long concrete motorway winding its way across the slumbering Pennines, with my father trapped inside the car as it sped towards the dark future. I did not cry. I sat numb, knowing that despite my compulsion, I could never become like him.

4

Life is suffering. This is the first of the Buddha's eternal noble truths. All my friends are burdened with remorse and regret. Nearly forty years old. Many of us possess neither money nor stability. We find ourselves as part of a decaying society. Unintegrated. Splintered. Our inner lives are tempestuous. Restlessness infects our being. There is no ground from which to take stock and evaluate our lives. Our grasp on the present is fragile. It is as if we are in stasis and the rotation of the earth has stopped. The days fly by, nothing new happens. There are only pseudo-problems, even eating is a chore. In the city, sunrise and sunset do not take place – we are not approaching death but are engulfed by it. The temptation is to escape into fantasy – close our eyes and wish the world would disappear. My friends and I are like children whose laughter has been censored. We are like crowns of wheat beheaded by a threshing machine. It's a strange catatonia. We are unable to move. Every decision we make is futile since we are limited to suffocating confines. Outside, there are meadows full of daisies unpicked, fields of pristine snow not trodden on, silent mountains where there are no echoes. The world is empty. There is no one. There is no us.

Sevim and I left Milton Grove and moved back into a one bedroom flat. We felt defeated and sad, although I was relieved to have been freed from the massive mortgage and have returned to a possibly simpler life. The grounds and walls of our house shook with the shriek of trains passing behind Rectory Road. Sevim found the noise troublesome. Her sleep was restive as she would often talk and turn in bed. I wished there was more I could do for her.

People still seemed strange to me. I wondered what their lives were like as I watched them passing by the house or lining up at the bus stop outside, waiting to head towards the city. Everyone seemed transfixed in a hermetic world.

'Work tomorrow, must sleep early, must iron my white shirt.'
'Hardly see you these days. We have to catch up.'
'Terrible thing happened to that boy.'
'Wonder if he'll like me?'
'What am I eating tonight?'
'It's not working. Just doesn't feel right.'

Every person I looked at seemed scared that life is short, despondent that it is far too long.

Like most people, I didn't want to show compassion to myself nor receive it from another. I tried telling myself 'Must remember that there are people who are fond of me and about whom I care'. I couldn't dare imagine a life where I might exist freed from anxieties, a place with children, and people loving each other. I told myself that the good life arises against the odds, from out the embers of a conflagrant system scorching the individual of dignity. It was difficult then for me to feel grateful for the friendships that survived – those people before whom I could be myself without feeling ashamed, but was too afraid to do so.

5

Though we seldom met, David and I had kept in touch through letters and the phone, ever since we were together in E53. I was glad when he decided to visit me with his lover, having heard of Sevim's and my troubles. He looked taller. The cobalt blue irises of his eyes looked as if they had been painted with a brush dipped in the diaphanous light of the soul. He sat beside Jonathan, his new boyfriend, at our dining table, which some poor tailor must have used over one hundred years ago to cut and sew clothes on. A picture of Durga looked on serenely – the invincible incarnation of the Great Mother carrying fearsome weapons in her many arms ready to slay. What was she thinking? I felt that her heart was beating with happiness in blessing. David had at last found equanimity. He was besotted with Jonathan who lacked nothing except charm. I couldn't help dislike Jonathan, not least because of his aloofness towards me, but also because he reminded me of a privet hedge: rather suburban and ordinary.

Jonathan felt threatened by David's affection for me. He showed this by taking issue with everything I said, just to show his intellectual superiority. It was just a way of controlling David who looked on him as the person who raised him out of the morass. Jonathan didn't allow him to have any independent thoughts – he critically scrutinised every word he said. I could see that David hadn't succumbed to domination. He just hid his strength better. He had made peace with his illness and with it came a sense of relaxed fortitude. I wondered to myself if he still retained his consummate courage to defend me.

We had had little time to ourselves. After dinner, Jonathan decided to go to bed early. When the cat's away the mice will play. David, Sevim, and I drank another bottle of red wine. There was a moment that David could not withhold his emotions any longer. He came over to the sofa where Sevim and I sat and, taking both our hands in his lap, he kissed me on my forehead.

'You're so lucky to be loved,' he said to me, 'But you think you don't deserve it, don't you?'

'Yes, I know,' I said. 'My illness has nothing to do with your friendship and love. I find the world cruel and unbearable.' I looked at the both of them feeling ashamed.

'You saw me once at a time when I wished I'd die quickly,' David said, his South Wales accent becoming rougher with the strength of his passion. 'But meetin' you changed all that. I saw in you a gentle, vulnerable man who epitomised a true spirit of love. And now I want to live long despite the AIDS that is killing my body. Trust me! You know, I've seen the cruelty of the world. You cannot teach love and the ways of angels to ignorant men. You're neglectin' the woman sitting next to you for a higher world that doesn't exist. You used to sing to me in your attic that we are born to this amazing life, and even if it became poison, then we'd have to drink it.'

'Are you trying to teach me responsibility?' I asked.

'No! No, dear friend. I'm askin' you to remember your voice again. I have felt the fire of your heart. Don't be afraid to love. What you give is enough and more,' he said.

'Michael, my love, if it makes you happy you should leave me,' Sevim said.

'What is happiness?' I asked. 'You've already sacrificed yourself for me. I am tired of your incessant giving. My body is tense with anger, because I have nothing to offer you that has any value. I know you don't intend it, but I feel inadequate in front of you both. Your ethical way of looking at life helps you exist in this world. You are both innocent. But I don't have such a persona, I have no ground to stand on from where I can call myself a man. You can't save me. It's patronising and cruel for you to even try. Maybe I want to be sick?'

*

Jonathan eventually became bored with David and they split up. My friend was bruised with rage. It was while he was travelling on a train that he became increasingly agitated conducting a fierce mental argument with his former lover. He began behaving erratically and to the concerned but afraid passengers, it was apparent that David was psychotic. He was sectioned and remained in hospital for several weeks. The psychiatrists prescribed olanzapine. Even now, our destinies seemed entwined since this was the same vile medication that I had been on before I began seeing Peter.

When I last saw David in the winter of 2006, we went to the market in Angel. The sun was shining and there was a brisk, keen air. He and I wandered aimlessly through Camden Passage, listening to the sounds made by people passing by. He was dressed in a long coat. Underneath, he wore a dark brown ribbed woollen jumper that expressed the gloom he was living in. 'I'm hungry,' he said after only a few minutes.

It wasn't a surprise even though we had had breakfast only about half an hour earlier. I knew that the tablets made you feel ravenous all through the day, and he had put on a lot of weight. His shoulders were hunched – as if he was carrying a mountain of sadness.

We headed towards Chapel Market. I wanted to take him to the Alpino, a 1960s Italian café I had accidentally seen one day. We went in – he liked the décor of orange light shades, wooden tables, and upholstered benches for seating. He ordered a full breakfast and I a coffee. We talked about the events leading up to his psychosis. He told me that he thought about suicide every day. He said his life wasn't worth living.

'You'll get better,' I kept reminding him, because it was what I felt I needed to hear at the height of my own crisis. I watched him eat – he played with the food on his plate in an uninterested way. All his senses had been numbed and he mourned the loss of his communicative, engaged, and vital self. We smoked and he insisted that I use his phone to tell Sevim where we were. He was trapped between wanting desperately to end his life and to live automatically for something without purpose.

We sat at the bus stop waiting to go to Camden. A Scottish man wearing short jeans with "love" and "hate" tattooed across the knuckles of his hands approached David. 'Can I have a cigarette, pal?' David fumbled his pockets; he had no more cigarettes left. He looked fearful. I took over. I rolled the man a cigarette. He was thankful and he asked, 'So you lads going out this evening for a couple of pints?' He was looking at David. I wanted to protect him, so I replied, 'No, we're having a quiet night in.' He told us that he was having six friends over at his small place in Tottenham, with some beers, to play cards for small change. 'It's just passing time isn't it? A bit of fun – not big money you see, just fun.'

It took a long time to arrive in Camden. The sky was grey, the light dull. It felt very cold. I was wearing my customary suede hat with its flaps folded down over my ears. David and I ambled through the crowds of vibrant young people, who all seemed to have the blood of life coursing through their bodies, still pursuing their dreams. He was walking in a different place. Care for the world around him and inner joy that used to light his face making it radiant had atrophied into despairing fear. We looked at leatherbound Indian notebooks, photographs, jewellery, stalls selling soaps, and incense. He phoned Jonathan. It was a quick call, probably just to hear his voice. Jonathan was brutal.

'Are you going to buy something for Jonathan?' I asked.

'He just wants porridge,' David said.

'Really?'

'You can't get it in Wales,' David replied, grinning. His sardonicism – a mixture of tired earnestness and bitterness – was stinging. 'Shall we have coffee?' he asked.

'Alright,' I said.

David insisted on treating me. His face momentarily lit up with the kindness I was accustomed to. I wanted this moment with my friend to last forever. But I couldn't help having a feeling of foreboding.

We stood outside a café, warming our hands around the cardboard coffee cups – for that time, at least, as we drank the coffee and smoked our cigarettes, standing silently, it felt completely natural and comforting. He had brought me out to Camden, and I was glad to be with him.

We walked, the crowds thicker now, the night air colder. I felt anxious for him walking beside me. On the way home, there was a Russian couple sat in front of us who talked animatedly with unceasing vigour for the entire hour on the bus. As we walked in the darkness across Stoke Newington Common, he said, 'I'm tired. I'll have a little rest when we get back.'

Three weeks later, David's sister called. He had died. He killed himself on a Sunday in the second week of February 2006. I still imagine the rope with which he hanged himself, hanging limply from the rafters of the loft where he lived and worked. He had been in torment. I hadn't understood how he was so very disconnected from the world around him, because of the effects of the medication – his hyper-anxiety, feeling of utter hopelessness at ever recovering from this episode, and the abject pain of Jonathan's rejection were scarring his body. In hindsight, I recall how he mostly sat quietly observing the scenes around him, not really participating, his mind distracted or perhaps engaged elsewhere at a distance from us. Sevim had loved him dearly. She had massaged his shoulders and felt bad that we could not offer him to stay longer, since our home was too small now. 'When I touched his body, it was like rock. He was very tense. There was nothing I could do to soften his muscles. He was really kind towards you and me. I'm so sorry we have lost him,' she said, letting her tears flow freely.

I phoned Sevim after David's funeral. It was a pitiful remorseless affair. His friends and relations, who I had never met before, were at the graveside. There was a sparse covering of snow on the muddy earth. Only David's mother was in deep grieving. The reverend's verse was well chosen and affecting. In a straightforward, unceremonious voice he read:

'For everything there is a season, and a time for every matter under heaven:

a time to be born, and a time to die;
a time to plant, and a time to pluck what is planted;
a time to kill, and a time to heal;
a time to break down, and time to build up;
a time to weep, and a time to laugh;
a time to mourn, and a time to dance...'

I had lost my friend. We had shared so much. It was beyond my comprehension how he, who had been such a beautiful being, could have turned his hand against himself. He had gone away. His suicide had settled deep in my blood and bones.

PART SIX

1

Early this morning my daughter, Hayal and I stepped into the garden; a spring sun shone in the sky like a daffodil. We listened to the birds talking to each other and believed we could understand them. They chirped and played in trees dressed with fresh buds. At the farthest hedge, a father blackbird was trying to feed a young chick that had fallen from its nest. The baby bird was hobbling along in the soil unable to fly. Sevim's instinctive need to rescue things took over. She rushed towards the little bird, with Hayal following close behind, and caught the fledgling in her hands. No sooner had she done this, the whole sky was filled with cries of alarm. The mother and father blackbirds swooped around Sevim's head, trying to retrieve their panic-stricken offspring. He curled up in a corner of the box we had put him in, his tiny body heaving with fear. I phoned a bird welfare line asking what to do. The parents had been trying to teach their child how to fly. Sevim felt dreadful. She set the bird loose where she had found it. I kept watch for cats as Sevim and Hayal left to go to the kindergarten. I felt upset.

An uncanny calm descended on our garden. There was still the commotion of birds, but they were in the distance in other gardens. I walked up to the spot where we had released the bird.

The poor little thing was cowering behind some ivy. I had this awful notion that perhaps we had accidentally sinned. Feeling forlorn, I lit a cigarette and put some music on the record player, to calm the distressed community of blackbirds. I sat looking and listening for over an hour hoping for a return to life. Then at last the father reappeared. He hopped down from the fence with a worm in his yellow beak to feed his son. My heart skipped. I felt joyful.

2

It's August 4th 2014, a languid afternoon. Our friends, Talya and Lewie with their daughter Maya; and Yifat and Peter with their daughter Hannah are visiting us from Israel. We are having a picnic on Hampstead Heath. I am lying on the grass dipping in and out of their conversation. We are concerned about the news which broke a few days ago that Israel is bombing Gaza.

Hayal and Maya, who are both seven years old, and Hannah, who is two years younger, are running through the long grass, trying to get a kite to fly. The grown-ups are eating and talking. I'm listening to the sound of the children's laughter, alert to their movements, looking at the trees, not wanting to participate in the conversation about Israel and Palestine because it disheartens me. Murder is being committed again. As a young idealist, I used to dream about mediating peace between the two peoples, even though I wasn't part of them. I grieved for Jews and Palestinians, the hundreds and thousands expelled from their homes, displaced and killed in conflict. I cared about what happened between Israel and Palestine, because my Sikh gurus had taught me to love humanity, fight oppression, and raise the downtrodden. Like Hayal, Maya, and Hannah playing in the grass, I too was around seven years old when I first awakened from my dream-state; my imagination was made aware of the barbarity of the world.

*

It was a summer's afternoon around 1973. My mother and I were alone. I was bored and she put on the television. I remember seeing monochrome images that seemed hyper-real. They were of men and machines clearing a mountain of human bones and corpses in a compound surrounded by barbed wire. A voiceover narrated what had occurred. My mother continued watching. She was unable to divert her attention from the horror, nor was she attuned to the effect the film may have on me.

'What's happening?' my mother asked. I did not know. I couldn't have guessed. Yet a primordial instinct told me these bones had belonged to people. My mother who had seen the dead many times couldn't recognise the inhuman scene.

'They are dead people,' I said.

'How did they die?' she asked.

'They gave them no food. And then they put them inside rooms where they couldn't get out, and then gas was given to them.'

'Who were killed? Who killed them?'

'I don't know, Mummy.'

'Listen more carefully. What is the television saying?'

'It's saying that the people who died were Jews.'

'What did they do?'

Feeling really emotional, I said, 'I don't know.'

'Why are their bodies being treated so badly?' she asked.

'Because they have no one left to care for them.'

There was a long pause. I was scared. The TV showed close-ups of survivors freed from concentration camps, harrowing faces looked straight at the camera.

'Will they do this to us?' my mother asked.

My mother began crying, her body heaving with the grief she felt. Compassion for humanity was moving her, but I wanted her to hug me, protect, and rescue me. She was mourning for those who had perished in the Holocaust. She was lamenting – crying for the world in which she had given me birth and where she knew that eventually I too would die.

I remembered this scene many years later when as a student I watched a discussion about the documentary *Shoah*. Professor George Steiner, who had lost many of his friends and family in the Holocaust and had spent a lifetime thinking about death, asked a question that entered my bloodstream. Close to tears but maintaining his dignity, Professor Steiner turned to the director Claude Lanzman with his voice breaking with sadness and said, 'Each time I witness a genocide, I become less human. The question is how far can we descend into the depths of Treblinka or Sobibor and still maintain our humanity?' I was ignorant about how to even begin answering this question; I didn't have even a language or words to describe the horror.

My mother held my hand; I walked in that field of death. There was not a sound. But it was not quiet. There was the whispering of trees, witnesses to the slaughter. They had become ill with what they had seen. Some emaciated men with shaven heads recited Kaddish. They stared at me. I was afraid of their look that begged to know if I was there as a murderer or as someone who would die with them.

Where was God? Heaven was empty. He was in the survivors' every sinew. He was in every word that issued from their mouths and in the warm breathing that blew out into the cold air. I'd made my choice. My mother put her hand on my head to comfort me as I lay motionless on my bed in E53 unable to live. My pillow was wet with saliva. My eyes hurting from uncried tears. The chosen people were put to death that day. They were dispatched without conscience. The Shoah is a laceration in every living soul. An eternal sorrow cannot wipe away mankind's vileness.

I have nothing; I know nothing. My heart knows desolation, because the idea of Israel as a place for humanity's confluence in fraternal love is shattered. The graceful men and women of every tradition on this earth have always claimed that there cannot be peace without freedom and justice – violence can never be a means of attaining this. The means always condition the ends – aggression always gives birth to hatred imprisoning one's humanity. Our children are playing in the grass. I wish they were ruling us with their purity and innocence.

Cold autumn winds are blowing across Britain. The warmth of the sun has receded into the folds of the earth. The long summer of 2014 is over. More than 2000 residents of Gaza were killed and about one hundred Israelis. Hamas had its day of martyrs. It is a shibboleth that Palestinian mothers dream of their sons to be carried aloft in coffins through the baking streets of Gaza and the West Bank, with their country folk crying hot tears for the dead. We know that the only real paradise of Allah is within people. A heart broken apart by grief is the real gateway to the divine. This earth, this scene, this body – is the only place where "Truth" becomes reality.

3

I bow humbly, seeking sanctuary at your blessed feet. Thou who art nameless and yet the artisan of all names. How can I praise thee who art formless and yet possess uncountable eyes and bodies? My voice is hushed, it trembles praising thy sword wielding mother and father. Your fearless love is unconquerable. You enter my being – my breath smells sweet like the eglantine raised by your hands. Holy Being, creator of day; arrester of night, anonymous and yet with attributes beyond my meagre capacity to enunciate. You are that which simply is. You are present as the meaning of every sentence. You are the ink in all writing, the voice of all that is spoken and sung. You are the ground, the salvation of all life. You meditate tirelessly in the darkest womb. You are Time, you are Death, you are the Feminine. From your mouth issues the music of the mountains and the scent of meadows. You command the suns and the light. You are your own Perfection. We who are nothing are brought to our knees in dread-filled supplication.

The mystery of my soul resonates in my heart and echoes endlessly round the circuit of a broken brain. I have arrived at a clearing in the middle of the world where I am again filled with a fever of compassion for everything that exists.

*

My daughter is asleep. I cooked haleem and chapatis this evening. While eating, she said, 'I'm never going to leave this house, even if I grow up and have ten children.'

'Where will they all sleep?' I asked.

'That's a good point,' she said.

After thinking a little while, she answered, 'We can all sleep in the same bed.'

4

I found growing up painful. It dawned on me slowly that all the conditioning that I took for granted had been false and outmoded. I never believed I would suffer repeated psychotic episodes. After every breakdown, a new journey had to begin by resolving or perhaps erasing the past. Each time, my will became weaker, making me detached, less interested in life.

I left my father. I must leave my mother. I remember her being old from the day she and I watched the documentary about the Holocaust. I felt ashamed. Maybe she was guilty for being unable to protect me. My boundless love for her felt unrequited. I missed my mother from her younger days. She worked in the Canada Dry bottling factory in the late 1960s. Her job was to lift bottles off a conveyor belt and put them inside empty crates, which she then lifted onto forklift trucks to be taken away and loaded onto lorries. She earned around £15 a week. She never found work dull. She was proud of what she did, having come from a village where women were confined to household chores and working in the fields. She was like a soldier – nothing could deter her from the jubilant feeling that she was contributing something vital to society.

She woke at 5am every morning. Made the fire. Then she would come to my bedside, lift my head, and make me drink a glass of warm milk. I used to fall back asleep immediately. After she left for work, I'd wonder where she had disappeared to. She had fantastic energy. She never complained about being tired, always tending to her family, cooking, cleaning, berating my sister's laziness. Her homecoming from work, which happened around 4:30pm, was always a beautiful sight. I would spot her in the distance in her long coat and headscarf, carrying her tiffin box, coming up Manor Drive – a hilly street lined with terraced houses where we lived. My mother felt part of the great adventure of being an economic migrant in the United Kingdom. She thanked God every day for giving her the chance to build a solid future without fear of poverty and destitution for her family. She threw herself into her new life with flamboyant dynamism, dedicating herself to sorting bottles with all her heart. She was tremendously grateful for the money she earned. Her eyes lit up, and she'd smile and marvel at the brown envelope containing her earnings. Going out to work was the most exciting period of my mother's life in Britain, and she never ceased from recounting it throughout her life.

On special days my mother used to oil and comb her hair back. She'd wear a flaming orange sari embroidered with silver sequins, her strong arms showing from beneath a short-sleeved blouse, an expression of indomitability sculpted on her face. Both she and my father were perfectly matched. Whenever they sat beside each other they exuded extraordinary charisma, holding an audience spellbound with the ease with which they spun captivating stories.

Our house was always full of people on Saturdays. Friends and relatives would converge and congregate for the weekend. The men would cook the meat and then sit down together to watch the wrestling, drinking whisky and rum, enjoying themselves, while the women caught up preparing the vegetable dishes. They made their own entertainment. My mother held court. She talked energetically, easily conjuring up the colourful atmosphere and memories of India, making everyone laugh with all their bellies or cry wistfully for the country they had lost and left behind. Perhaps I'm being romantic, but I remember the community of my parents' generation having an amazing sense of purpose that their children could never hope to emulate. As a child, there was a fragile harmony in my living between a mythical India and my home here in Britain. It was only much later that I became divided and anxious about where I belonged.

I spoke with my mother on the telephone. Her voice was old and cracked, a remnant of a bygone age where people were more in touch with the nature around them. An unending spectrum of distilled and unrefined feeling is contained in her voice: remorse, anger, happiness, hope, disappointment, determination – I can't exactly tell when my mother is saying something joyful or tragic.

'I saw two angels last night,' she said.

'What do you mean?' I asked.

'Don't you know what angels are?'

'No. There are no such things.'

'You saw them when you were in the mental hospital.' It was true.

'Where did you see them?'

'On the television. There was a room with four doors – two angels stood there and they talked to me. One was young wearing white clothes. He was surrounded with a golden light. His eyes were bright. He told me, "Michael needs to give in to the depression." He told me that you will find the fire from which creation is born. My son, I believed the angel. He talked about a renewal and said, "Your son will meet himself and he will meet the God he believes has died".'

'What did the other angel say?' I said.

'I didn't care much for him. He told me that you had become old and bitter. Is it true, Michael, that you no longer believe in anything? Are you resentful of your parents or losing Anarkali? You have a virtuous and beautiful wife now, what is there to be sad about?'

Ever since my father died, my mother's family, including me, had increasingly pushed her to the margins. She kept herself isolated in her room and was beginning to hear things on the radio and see things on television that were not there. I had loved my mother insanely and now felt guilty for not being able to make her last wishes to live with Sevim and me come true. I don't think she understood; she was broken-hearted by my rejection. My sickness had become an easy excuse to keep away and here she was giving me hope by telling me about her angels. Today, she sounded like a sweet girl. She wanted me to believe that she was fine and could look after herself.

I wished she would just say, 'Michael, why don't you love me anymore. I am sad and alone, I want to come and live with you.'

She worries about who will look after her when she becomes even less mobile or perhaps even bedridden. She prays that God keeps her moving until her last breath. She prays for an early painless death even though it scares her. I wish I could return her sublime love.

There's no one I can turn to. Life has been a torture ever since God has been defeated in my soul. Like fields wet with morning dew, so my waking and sleeping is sprinkled with loneliness and haunting anxiety. I do not recognise the animal I have become. My humanity has shrivelled in the face of maturity. All of the constellations that guided my paths in life have clouded over; the world of brittle ideas which was the foundation of my existence has imploded. I am living without hope: a paper boat tossed about on the surface of an untameable sea.

5

I often felt my love for Sevim was not strong enough to carry me through my difficult convalescence. My ego didn't allow her caring to take seed in my being. For months, she woke up without me, spending hours by herself doing things around the house then going to work. It was as if I had abandoned her. My energy was low. I couldn't throw aside my heaviness and embrace her completely as my heart desired. I seemed to want a different life. I was displeased with my image. I fantasised about being courageous; picking up my coat, leaving my possessions, and withdrawing completely from her. I needed to be alone – and that was my real fear.

Morning was the time that I felt the side effects of the tablets most acutely: a mouth like sandpaper, hot and cold sweats, dizziness, restless breathing, palpitations. I was uncertain about the future. I wanted to be unconscious and sleep forever. I was too sick to wish anything else. I felt uncomfortable with everything around me. Things seemed unfamiliar to me, as if I was encountering them for the first time. Sometimes I was compelled to point out and name the most mundane object for myself. I occupied myself by saying something silently like 'that's a kettle' or 'that's a table', which brought a momentary ease but also exhaustion. I was out of place. My senses had been completely dulled and I could not grasp life.

I watch Sevim painting our bedroom window. I remember we used to play together. In those depressing times, we weren't keeping much in each other's company. She was lonely. I, on the other hand, was constantly preoccupied with what is invisible – transcendental questions about God, the purpose of existence and what, if anything, is meaningful. I was obsessively anxious always about how we were going to survive and then there was decaying state of the planet.

While seeing Peter, I began writing my reflections and feelings about being ill which became a channel for self-healing and catharsis. Having written a few words, I felt rested. With all my complaints on a page I would in a strange way begin to look forward to the day, another moment on my journey from darkness to light.

*

On that translucent summer's day when I had left Sevim to go to work and experienced the breaking of my psyche, the branches of the London plane trees swayed rhythmically as if fanning the world in adoration. I could see the horse chestnut trees that were prematurely in autumn flame because an insect had laid its pupae on their leaves – so green was flecked with burnt browns, summer melded with autumn. It was then that I felt I had come across some occult truth. In the Garden of Eden, there were two trees: the Tree of Knowledge of Good and Evil from which we ate and the Tree of Life which was lost to us. That day I was in ecstasy because I felt I had rediscovered the Tree of Life; its roots were in my soul and its branches descended down to sorrowful earth – I was that tree.

One day in the middle of being ill, soon after I'd started seeing Peter, I was in Clissold Park. It began raining. I walked slowly looking at the coots and moorhens scuttling to-and-fro between the grass and ponds on which the raindrops fell and the swans and ducks happily swam. There was nobody there except the animals and me, and I was, for a moment, relieved of the fear of dying that I carried in my heart. I knew somehow that I would be born again. This was a day of redemption for losers like me. It felt like a carnival where all the rhetoricians were being judged by a higher power – people like Blair who spoke with great finesse misleading people to accept untruths and making acceptable the deplorable. I smiled, knowing nothing could ever justify the death and pauperisation of millions of human beings.

6

I had put my mother in her wheelchair and was pushing her along rugged paths through the playing grounds towards the wood. I had come to visit her from London, and she couldn't stop beaming her glowing smile, with her oversized false teeth. It had been three months since I'd seen her, even though I was unemployed and had nothing better to do with my time than to think. My arms and legs felt weak because of the medication I was on but was glad to be outside with her. I'd draped her favourite grey paisley embroidered shawl around her shoulders and she was holding the walking stick I had bought for her from Covent Garden. We were passing beside a gurgling stream and stopped to take a rest. She praised the dragonflies and butterflies for their beauty. They gave her immeasurable happiness.

I sat down beside her wheelchair, my hand resting on her frail legs. 'How long do I have to live?' she asked.

'I don't know. No one can know the time,' I said.

'But you read the papers. Surely they must write something about my dying.'

'The papers only report news about famous people.'

'I raised and educated you. How come you don't know when I will die? Are you hiding the truth from me?'

'No, Mummy. You've taught me that everything is subject to Waheguru's will. We have to obey whatever is his command.'

'I care for Him, as much as I care for you. I think I've got a long time to live. I'm not ready to go until I've seen your child.'

'I'm not sure if Sevim and I can have children.'

'Your father would just so much as smile at me, and I would become pregnant,' she said and bursting out laughing.

It was my mother who taught me that the world is steeped in the psyche. Every event that takes place outside, like the waning and waxing of the moon, a star shooting across the night sky, the rising and setting of the sun, the opening of buds on trees and shoots appearing through the soil as spring wakens once more – these things also take place inside consciousness. All matter and incarnation of life is psychical. The story of the origins of the universe is the same as the birth of consciousness. I needed my mother to be immortal.

I imagine, just after creation when there was still darkness. Animals and man slept in the lap of my mother whose nature was impenetrable mystery. She dreamt the lives and fate of her children, lulled them in their visions in which God appeared and spoke to their souls. For thousands of years, it rained on the earth; night followed day, the mountains stood mightily gazing heavenwards as the milky way swirled in ecstasy, the seas rocked against the shores of sleeping continents. Still there was no beginning, only the mesmeric play of numinous forces. There was immense love and hope, longing and unbound desire in the original meditation and thought that was the source of creation. The seed had been sown, but the womb still had not given birth to life.

The earth waited submerged in oceans. Warm and cool, turbulent and placid winds blew across the deluge. Light fell on the surface and was absorbed by the darkness. Infinity, which existed before even space existed to hold the worlds and their constellations, metamorphosed itself into a cloth and wrapped itself around the entire cosmos. My mother withdrew into herself to brood upon her children and reflect on the enigma of her own origins. She had emerged out of the Divine to quell his loneliness. In a night, she became both his daughter and his wife. 'What is the nature of this law, whereby I was set free? Who is that Being which wills itself to be known only to shatter the mirrors in which he looks?' She thought deeply to the end of time.

PART SEVEN

1

Hayal, daughter, your birth changed everything for me. You were conceived between the 8th and 11th of July 2006. That year, there had been very strange weather. The leaves did not appear on the trees until the middle of June. There had even been snow in May, so summer was very late in coming. Your mother and I had not been trying very long for a baby. We went to a concert of Sufi Muslim music in Regent's Park in the shadow of the mosque. It was wonderful. Amongst the singers was the Qawali group, the Mansour Brothers, from Pakistan. We had met them a few years before when they were last at the Sacred Voices Festival. Your mother bought them wine and we became friends carousing through the evening, breaking the taboos of strict Islam.

The day in the park was hot and sunny. I danced a whirlwind in the grey evening. Listening to our friends singing ecstatically the praises of Imam Ali, I felt the Invisible Divine moving through the trees. The branches were bowing and every leaf seemed emblazoned with Allah's name. Sevim and I stood hand-in-hand, looking at the clouds disappearing beyond a horizon of high-rise buildings and feeling really happy.

Your mother was worried about whether we would ever be able to have a child. Her fears, as you now know, were unfounded.

But you will also discover that sometimes when people are very close, they can make each other's anxieties seem bigger than they actually are. Reality is often simpler than what we imagine. Your mother was worried about her age – sometimes she dreaded it was too late to start a family. On the other hand, I too was unsure because I felt God had not been kind to us.

One day, a long time before your conception, I entered a church called St Augustine's near Highgate. It was around Easter and the furniture was covered with cloths. Outside was a damp cold evening. It was dark inside the church. There were only two other people there. I knelt in front of a sculpture of Mary holding Christ's limp body and lit a candle. Only death hung above his face and the scene was made heavy by a mother's grief for her son. Mary's maternal instincts had not yet allowed her to forgive Christ for choosing to die and without her human mercy, he would not be able to rise again and attest to his truth of being God incarnate. I lowered my head and prayed desperately for your mother's dearest wishes to come true. I wanted only her happiness and nothing for myself.

*

Your mother, as you know, can be a little inquisitive. She asks many questions of herself and life, takes action and wants answers quickly. She thought she might be pregnant and wanted to prove it, even though it had been less than a month. But as usual, I disagreed and wanted to wait before finding out. Your mother became angry; we argued in the middle of the street. I felt regretful so I sheepishly went to the Benjamin Pharmacy on the high street and bought a pregnancy kit. I walked back through the empty playground of a local council estate, feeling a little low. When I got back, your mother was sleeping so I woke her up and we made up. Then she went to the bathroom and used the pregnancy stick.

'Michael,' she said calmly. 'A pink stripe has come up.' She smiled from cheek-to-cheek. Her intuition had been correct

– you were already inside her tummy. We hugged and kissed each other. Then I lit a cigarette to think about what had just happened.

*

Your mummy and I were over the moon with joy. We were filled with love for you, even before seeing you. And yet sometimes, my darling, happiness and pain are not so different from each other. Your daddy is very easily affected by joy and sadness. Little things make me laugh and cry. If I experience this too much, I can become poorly. Knowing you were going to be born moved me deeply. It was a bit like an earthquake.

I had to leave your mummy to go to Leeds to try and sort out some messy family business. While I was there, I still had time to go into the woods where I used to wander after school and think about my life. I sat by the river, looking at the lush green foliage, listening to the whirring of insects and seeds bursting out of their pods. The sun was dancing off the water. The light was moving gently up the tree trunks in waves. The leaves were dappled in shade and sunlight. It was a real magical garden. I hope it doesn't sound too strange but I began crying happy tears. I was glad about you – even the nature around me was in bliss. But I felt very solitary. I thought about the heartbreaking love between King Lear who became mad and his daughter Cordelia. Because of my history with psychosis, I identified with Lear. I had an intimation that yours and my relationship – still in its genesis – would be punctured by tragedy. Perhaps I was just sad about feeling incapable of being a good father. I had neither a job nor money and felt there was nothing I could give you. It was silly but I couldn't help it.

When I got back home to London, the strength of my feelings made me become ill. It wasn't so bad. But because your mummy really loves me, she was very worried and upset. It was the first month of her pregnancy and I wasn't going to be around to help much. For the next three weeks, I would wake up early in the morning and walk up Stoke Newington Church Street past the closed shops and cafes, around Clissold Park four or five times, where I'd talk to the trees, plants, and birds. They would respond by waving and talking to me. Your mother didn't want me drawing attention to myself on the street, so whenever I felt the urge to sing out loud, I would put on my earphones and listen to music on my Walkman. Back in our flat, I was cleaning, cooking, talking with myself, and dancing in the kitchen in celebration and anticipation of your imminent appearance in the world. Soon I was feeling much better.

*

You are a miracle in our lives. Sometimes, when your mother cradles you in her arms while feeding you day and night, her body is tense as she resists conflicting emotions knocking on the door of her mind threatening to consume her rationality. Nothing is allowed to get in the way of her caring for you. I am so moved by your every small expression and vulnerability in this world. At one month, you made beautiful sounds, trying so hard to talk to us. What were you trying to say? I wish you were able to tell us what it was like in your mummy's womb. Maybe you were just fascinated by the luminescence of the things surrounding you? Whatever it was, your being made opposites hang harmoniously together and transcending dreams appear real.

Every newborn arrives with the mystery of existence. For your mother, there has been a renaissance of trust in the world. The wise men in ancient India said that Enlightenment was to stop longing for love. Well, my daughter, your love is endless and there isn't a need to think beyond the delight I experience looking at you.

*

I see your mother sitting half up in bed holding you close to her chest because you have gas. She will sleep like this with you, through the dark night until the birds wake up in the morning. She will be with you completely, visualising your every dream, listening to your every need and wish. It is beautiful to watch her with you. And it is breathtakingly wonderful to see her pour herself into you. She is no longer just Sevim. In my mind, she becomes like the fearless goddess Durga, who lives inside the forests, rests in mountains and inside the silent earth, caring for all sentient beings of this creation. You love being close, smelling her breasts like a rose. And the sounds you make show us that you are happy.

*

Photographs from the time when your mummy was carrying you in her tummy don't capture the way she really was. Imagine the loveliest smile in the whole world that gives you the feeling of blossom falling from trees. Look in the mirror and see yourself laugh – that's how wonderful she was. Words and language are not so good at showing what we experience as human beings. I will never forget how incredibly joyful, exhilarated, and delightful she looked as she was wheeled out of the operation theatre holding you. The hospital corridor was empty. The sun shone through the windows. The nurse had already said, 'Congratulations, you're the father of a beautiful daughter.' I was in shock. And then I saw you both. It seemed both of you were covered in a halo of light, just like the pictures of Mary and Jesus. Inside, I felt crushed. I didn't know what to do. There were thousands of tears, but they remained inside me. I was mesmerised by what I saw.

My darling Hayal and darling Sevim, in the end I fear I let both of you down.

2

The summer of Sevim's pregnancy was tranquil and bright. We used to go for walks along Church Street, watch television and listen to songs by Baris Manco, Eva Cassidy, Simon and Garfunkel or Indian music. We listened to a lot of radio. One of the very moving pieces of classical music we heard was 'The Fall of a Leaf' by Imogen Holst. The contemplative mournful cello was like a gentle hand comforting our waiting for the birth.

Sevim was in a sensitive mood. She felt fragile and was easily moved. It had been the bicentenary of the abolition of the slave trade in England and this historical event was being marked by celebrations. One morning, while having breakfast, we heard a radio documentary about how a very rich man who owned slaves set them free. Sevim began weeping – her eyes flowing with big tears. She was crying because there are good people in the world who stand up for their ideals and also because of the cruelty one person can inflict on another human being.

It was a halcyon period. We sensed the effortless passage of time. Sometimes, we met Sevim's sisters and brother Murat. Occasionally, Talya and Lewie popped over. People drifted in and out of our small flat. When I look back, I see that we were happy deep down.

Autumn approached. There was some anxiety about how we would greet our new guest. Our house was too small and not so comfortable. So we decided to build an extension and have it decorated. It would take a long time.

It is one of the most beautiful things on Earth that God gives every creature a home. All the birds in the world have their nests. All the animals on the earth have a place to live – except we are determined to destroy nature and their environments. It is also very sad that so many people in this society are homeless. Why do so many people have nowhere to live? It's a shame. People from the oldest cultures of the world, like the Australian Aborigines and Native Americans, all used to have a place to live. Don't we think everyone should have a place they call home?

The Polish men who did the work were decent honest people. They were like angels, because they cared about us and were providing us with what we needed without charging too much money. It was great fun watching them work. They listened to classical music while labouring in the middle of mess: shifting rubble, nailing, drilling and hammering, painting the walls.

We moved back to our house even though the work was still incomplete. There was a big hole in the living room floor, since the basement was also being dug to create more space. So we had only our bedroom and kitchen. But we were happy and at ease. We woke up every cold winter's day at 5.30am. One morning, we saw a bright ochre sky and it was snowing. I got up and made coffee listening to music. I was imagining playing in the garden with our daughter in the snow, in the future to come. Then at about 7 am, Costek, one of the workers, arrived. He drank black coffee with six sugars. We smoked and talked over our hot drinks, about life's difficulties on this very peaceful day.

189

3

I remember it was a warm April afternoon. The sun shone in a brilliant cloudless sky. Time had slowed down. These were going to be the last hours before you entered the world. On the table in the kitchen was a bowl of fruit and vase of flowers. A light breeze blew through the patio doors that opened onto the garden. It was fragrant. The radio was on playing classical music. It could have been the fourth movement of Mahler's Symphony Number 5, brimming with melancholy. Sevim was taking photographs while Leyla and I were washing and drying the floor on our knees. She captured us looking up at the camera, smiling and laughing, full of happiness and giddy anticipation.

The washing had been taken down from the line except for two dishcloths which swayed gently in the air. I stood in the garden with my arm around Sevim's shoulder. It looked like we were marrying each other again, or meeting after a long time or perhaps preparing to say goodbye. This was a wonderful odd moment, knowing that tomorrow, two would become three.

Sevim hadn't slept for the last two nights. I was on a mattress on the floor. When the pain of her contractions became too intense, she would get up from her bed, trying not to disturb me, and walk around the flat. In my own half sleep, I dreamt or perhaps even saw your mother's father coming into the room to comfort his daughter. He was wearing a trilby hat, and he raised his hand as if to bless her. It was soothing to know that he was around, looking after both his daughter and granddaughter to be.

*

I held Sevim's hand and was tearful. She told me not to worry. She told me that she and our baby would be fine. I only had to look after myself. Then we were ready to go to the hospital. I had to leave her beside her bed, and as I walked out with Nejat to the car, I could not help but feel that I had forgotten something. It was sad leaving her alone and vulnerable. Maybe she needed to reassure our child that the world was not such a bad place to live in.

I went home and lay on the sofa. I began watching a Tibetan film about young monks desperate to watch the football World Cup on television in their monastery. It was a joyful film about how the world is changing rapidly, how ancient traditions have something profound to teach us but must also adapt. It was a strangely lovely film to start seeing, because the biggest change in our lives was about to happen. Then at 11pm, Leyla called. Sevim had gone into labour.

4

I put on my brown furry Kashmiri hat – my security against the weather and the world – and waited outside the house. It was very quiet and the night air was misty. There was even a light drizzle, a blessing from heaven. Leyla pulled up in a taxi in front of the house, I jumped in and we were driven to the hospital. The journey seemed to take forever. I remember being wrapped up in my own world looking out of the window as we passed the estates, Victorian houses, and shops of Hackney, praying silently for Sevim and my daughter's protection and hoping the revolution to a new life would be peaceful.

We got out at Homerton Hospital. A few people and patients in their pyjamas were just hanging around outside or smoking. The place felt oddly lonely. A cold wind blew through the car park. Leyla and I walked down the long empty corridor and up the stairs to the labour room. Sevim was standing against the bed, rocking from left to right. She was in a lot of pain but was strong like a tree and determined to push Hayal out into the world. We were all very eager to see our new daughter, child, and friend.

The nurses told us that our child would be born around six o'clock in the morning. Hours passed without any progress and still Hayal hadn't entered the world. Sevim remained calm and focused on delivering her child. Leyla and I felt helpless not knowing what to do. It was all too much for us in the dimly lit room.

Eventually, I phoned the doula. Matilda was an Orthodox Jewish woman who was a few months pregnant herself. I was supposed to have called her earlier but didn't feel comfortable doing this, so late in the night in the middle of the Sabbath, even though she had told us that she would be present whenever was necessary. True to her word, Matilda was with us within an hour, all the way from Enfield. As soon as she entered dressed elegantly, a calmness came to the room. Leyla and I felt relieved and stepped out into the early morning light to have a coffee and something to eat. I was feeling tired and run down and asked to go home to sleep.

*

The ringing of the phone woke me up. It was Saturday afternoon. The sun shone brightly. I rushed to the hospital. They had already taken Sevim into the operating theatre. I sat beside Leyla in the waiting room. She was crying a lot. She couldn't believe the effort her sister was going through. 'When I see that little baby, I'm going to smack her bottom,' she said. She was also upset with Sheriban and Gulsum who had turned up late. Everyone sat quietly, hardly looking at each other. We were all worried.

5

My dear Hayal, you arrived at 16:23 on Saturday 14th April 2007. It was the most wondrous precious moment of your mother's and my life. Matilda gave you over to your mummy who kissed and fed you – they say you were really hungry.

I stood looking at you with your little hat on, trying to understand who you were and how you had come to be with us bringing all the peace, love, and beauty of life. Nothing could describe your being. It was foolish even to try. My mind felt heavy. My heart ached. Emotions and intuition, my love – being close to you was what was needed. My cheek against your cheek, my love openly flowing to you, smelling and feeling your presence in this world created specially for you. That would have been a true moment. Instead, I was mute. Unable to know what to say and unaware of what I was feeling.

*

Thinking about birth raises questions about life and death. What is truth? What is reality? Albert Einstein said that everything is relative. No one knows everything. My darling Hayal, you were coming from a space like infinity. When I looked into your mummy's blazing eyes, she was totally connected with your universe and God guiding you into our arms. On the other hand, I was lost somewhere. I was just amazed and tired from witnessing the mystery unfold.

On the third day after your birth, I had a severe psychotic lapse. In the days leading up to your being born, I prayed passionately for too long.

One only sees someone or something when it has been looked at twice. That I suppose can also be called relativity. The second time I looked at you was when I visited you from my hospital. It was the first time I really saw you. I picked you up and held you to my chest. You lay your cheek on my shoulder and rested as if you had known me a hundred years. From that moment, I felt a torrent of love. I felt your breath on my neck. I smelt you. The care that came from you made the hair on my arms stand straight. There were no polar opposites. Everything felt whole and one. I promise always to remember this and love you. Believe me.

Lovingly, your father.

6

The sun was glowing as if we were in a desert. There were pink clouds in the sky that early evening. Nejat and I had come to bring Sevim and Hayal from Homerton Hospital. We were walking through a morass of poverty in this enclave of London. My heart was sinking with the feeling that so many of the sick were poor. I felt upset that children here and everywhere in the world would be dying because of deprivation, of how we had stolen their lives.

How is this possible? It is because we don't take responsibility for our humanity, preferring to give it away to people who make excuses and justify the way we survive without understanding or feeling. Others are belittled and cast aside in a story which justifies the power of the wealthy and the distress of the poor. The balance between rulers and subjects is said to be decided by an invisible hand of an omniscient god. I don't believe such a god ever existed.

Over the last twenty-four hours, Hayal's birth had gently but dramatically begun excising the political fabric and structures of my mind.

I sat on the bonnet of the car parked outside the hospital. I watched people of every race, colour, and creed coming and going from the hospital. I felt that I was the richest man in the world. God had delivered Hayal to us, along with uncountable wishes. Unlike in fairy tales, I didn't want to use them wisely. I wanted to wish only with love.

Sevim and Gulsum had been waiting patiently with Hayal on the ward. Nejat and I arrived late. Quietly, I began leading the way back out of what appeared to me to be a maze. Hayal had come from the protected encampment of the womb, and this would be the first time she would be experiencing being outside in the spring breeze and mellow sunshine. I was unable to contain my feelings. Everyone was worried.

Sevim asked Nejat to pull up the car around the corner from the hospital in an empty, decrepit estate. We sat silently. The whole world seemed to be sanctified by Hayal's presence. For me, the soul of God had descended and my unhappy life was now complete. There were pigeons scavenging for food. In front, I focused on a cherry tree that had burst out in blossom from the cold night before when it had stood bare looking star-wards. I imagined I could see God's soul playing amongst the swaying branches, petals of blossom floating placidly to the ground as an offering of prayer. I was speechless.

7

Sevim and Hayal had only been home for a day, maybe two. Many friends and well-wishers had come to the house to congratulate us. My mind couldn't stop skipping and running because I was afraid of losing our child. I couldn't stop visualising the inhuman ways in which black people, immigrants, the mentally ill, disabled, and Jewish people had been treated. I was aware only of Hayal's fragility, and of how we could get caught in the currents of a savage river of human despair and suffering. A voice, my own most precious voice, said to me, 'This has to stop. We must protect the vulnerable and weak.'

I lay down in the garden on a heap of clippings and branches and looked up at the starless sky. I imagined there was a white man, a top secret agent sent to safeguard my family, who had taken a drug to change his colour so that he could blend in, and no one would know the difference. I could hear a conversation taking place between the secret agent and his boss.

'Wow. I never knew Indians, Kurds, and black people had families, such wonderful love and care between them. What are they celebrating?' asked the secret agent.
    'They're celebrating the birth of a daughter,' said the boss.
    'Then why is the father so distressed?'

'He's worried he won't be able to protect her and let her lead the life she deserves in this society.'

'Why, what has he done wrong?'

'He's mentally ill. And he comes from a background where he and his kind have been judged by the colour of their skins and the prejudices of ignorant people.'

'Isn't it a little overdramatic of him? Isn't he jeopardising the life of his daughter by being unduly negative?'

'He's concerned about what antipathy and ignorance give birth to. He's worried about the infernos of hatred unleashed by societies on their neighbours, brothers and sisters, like for example in Rwanda, Nazi Germany, and state-sanctioned lynchings of slaves and free Africans in America.'

'I think I'm beginning to understand. After all, I'm a black man now.'

'No, stupid. You're white. You've just taken some drugs to make you look black. Your empathy doesn't extend so far that you can actually understand what this father experiences. Besides you're just a secret agent sent to protect this family.'

'From what?'

'Just in case Michael's ruminations might be correct.'

'What do you mean? I thought he's mad. Insane. Sent over the edge by the birth of his daughter.'

'His belief is so strong that he might be prepared to die so that the world might be a better place for his daughter and all the children who are born here.'

'That's very noble, but the kingdom of God wasn't even founded with Christ.'

'Very good, secret agent. Maybe you are beginning to understand after all. However, we fear that should he die, his vision of a better world would die with him, and we would be left at the mercy of a fictional god and his crazy timeframe. I mean who would wait more than 2000 years for the return of a man who was definitively crucified? That's nonsense. But we also fear that should Michael live, then his yearning for a life of salvation for all might also be realised, and we cannot abide that either. People are not ready for it.'

'In other words, you want this man, what's his name, yes, Michael, not to die and you don't want him to live either.'

'Yes.'

'So how am I supposed to protect him and his family? What's my mission?'

'Simply let him go mad.'

'But wouldn't that be letting down all these beautiful people who are here celebrating just a happy birth? As far as I can see this man is just a normal man, and his friends and family are just like my own.'

'You're beginning to ask too many questions, secret agent. Best leave the discussions about virtue and ethics to us. And besides they're not like you or your network. They're black and remember, you're white.'

'Now look here. He's looking really distressed. He just wants us to leave him alone. Can't we just do that little thing?'

'No, secret agent.'

'But I feel he's a good guy?'

'He's a threat to our existence.'

'But we are the ones who killed his people. We are the oppressors and they are the oppressed. Can't we leave this family alone?'

'No. Just remember secret agent, you're a white guy acting black. There's nothing you can do for them. There's no one who can help him. He shouldn't have messed with men like Tony Blair.'

*

When I had been unable to stop the conversation between the secret agent and his boss, I became erratic and began pacing around the garden. Then I began to think something bad was going to happen to Sevim and to Hayal. I started to run towards the kitchen and went straight into the doors. My frightened niece Angie, and Sevim's eldest sister Sheriban dragged me into the house screaming, kicking and shouting. I lay on the floor crying inconsolably. Sevim, who had been looking after our baby appeared. She bent down and put her hand on my chest. I felt her care and need to protect me, and our child. I began trying to relax beneath her touch. 'You're not well, Michael. You've become ill. Please be still. We have a child to think about,' she said comforting me. Then she phoned the police trying to explain what was occurring. It was depressing to think that I had become a danger to myself and perhaps even others.

*

It was a damp night. An ambulance and the police waited outside to put me in handcuffs. I was resisting going into the back of the police van. I was terribly afraid – scared like an insect caught in a spider's web. I did not want to live and I wanted to live. I did not want to die but I wanted to die. My mind did not know which way to turn. The silence that rests in every human being had awakened inside me. And all I wanted was noise.

*

'Sir, I can't let this go on. I'm prepared to protect this man with my life,' said the secret agent.

'Nonsense. You are this man,' the boss said.

'But I'm a white secret agent pretending to be black.'

'You've become this man. There isn't a single real person with enough compassion to save him from his agony.'

'So who is he and who am I?'

'You are invisible. And he is you.'

'Then his daughter is mine. She can't become an orphan. I have to survive.'

'That's correct. But he must die or become insane.'

I was exhausted from kicking the sides of the police van. 'Let me go. Let me go,' I screamed.

'Can you calm down?' one of the police officers asked. 'Do you know where you are?'

'I have to leave you now,' the secret agent said to me. 'Maybe there is at least one person you trust who can save you?'

'Stupid,' the boss said. 'Finish him off.'

I was looking out of the rear window of the police van and could see Murat and his friend Kagan on the street wondering what was going on. The neighbours were also out, some were looking through their windows.

I was terrified. Then I called on Peter in my mind to appear. He was sat comfortably in his library, with a glass of red wine, placed on a side table. I bowed my head, and said, 'Peter, can you help me?'

'What ails you, Michael?' he asked.

'My heart is heavy. The birth of my daughter has awakened a love inside me that is too heavy to bear. My world is overflowing with wickedness. I want the monstrous events to end, and the lives of all those who have been tortured or killed to be redeemed so that when she grows up and asks, "Where did you stand, Daddy?" I will be able to answer, "Alongside the Truth".'

'That's beautiful, Michael. May I look into your heart?'

Peter's spirit then entered my body and he felt the pain and saw the desolate emptiness. He heard the cries of children and smelt the funeral fumes of the cremated dead. He lifted his glass to drink.

'No, Peter. The wine contains poison!' I shouted.

There was a smile on his face but his eyes looked unhappy.

'Fuck it. There are some things worth dying for,' he said, and drained the goblet.

I heard a great sound of shattering glass in my head. I sat down in the back of the police van and sat there mourning my friends.

8

It was with great irony that I was returning to the hospital where just hours before I had picked up Hayal's fragile being. The drive to Homerton seemed to last forever.

'He seems to have calmed down now,' I heard one of the policemen say to the other. Then he looked back at me, 'Feeling any better?' he asked.

I felt heartbroken and sad. The three of us sat in a private waiting room for the doctors and social workers to assess me. On the wall were two paintings of some American West Coast city like Los Angeles or San Francisco. In one, there was a jazzy sun shining at dusk; in the other, it had melted and given way to the moon.

Eventually, I was admitted onto a psychiatric ward. It was an unwelcoming place. In the main communal room where patients gathered, there were blue leather sofas, a pool table, and some tables and chairs for us to sit at when eating or meeting visitors. Mounted in the centre of the main wall was a large television screen protected inside a Perspex box, so no one could smash it. The television was on all the time, and whoever could find the remote control commanded the atmosphere on the ward. There was a small selection of books which no one read. The Bible, however, was copiously underlined and defaced. On one of the walls, the word "YOU" was painted in large capital letters, which I found really oppressive. I tried to avoid going to the toilets as much as I could because they had no seats. I complained to one of the nurses about it and he explained that they had been removed because they were being smashed repeatedly, as well as the fact that they could be used as a weapon. The showers were filthy and on at least one occasion, a patient had defecated in one of them. At eating times, we jostled in line beside the kitchen, waiting for the shutters to go up. We all ate as if we had never been fed and this would be the last meal we ever would see again.

I spent the next eighteen days there.

Many of the patients were very hurt people and because of this, some of them seemed pretty scary. My brothers visited me as did Leyla. I just sat, not really wanting to talk much. Sevim reminded me that I called her on the phone, beseeching her in my drugged up low voice: 'Please, darling, get me out of here.'

There were no recreational facilities in this hospital, but I was lucky that I had a private room. Actually, I was glad. I did not want to sleep on the ward, which felt very unsafe.

There was someone I was missing terribly. It was a more severe heartache than any I had ever experienced. The pain I felt was intense and searing. The whole world seemed a flood of sorrow. Hayal was so close and so far away. I hadn't even held her properly or called out her name. For so many months, we had been together while she had worked towards life hidden in her mother's womb. Now that she had entered this world where finally I could see her, we were separated. I felt terribly unworthy to be in Hayal's presence, perhaps even ashamed to call myself her father. In the afternoon on the ward, the other patients would look at me as I walked up and down, cradling a blanket in my arms as if it were my baby.

I wasn't allowed out and I didn't want to watch television, so I spent most of my time smoking in what was called the Quiet Room, where the radio was constantly on through big speakers, blaring out soul, reggae, and hip hop. Sometimes, one of the patients would get up and dance. There was Andrew, a handsome black man; Junior, whose hands shook as he chain smoked with cuts all down his arm; and Gloria, whose wig moved around her head every time she scratched it. It was like sitting in the waiting room of a dirty train station, except that there was nothing outside.

I don't believe people really die. We become someone's Past. We continue to abide in the memories of loved ones. Our refreshed souls enter and are reborn in the Future. As human beings, we seem only able to exist in the Past and Future. The Present may be an irredeemable instant. Please don't be scared if I say I had died. I was in what Buddhists call a Bardo, a passing state, an interval between two worlds. Everywhere I looked, I saw emptiness and loneliness. Once again, I had returned to the point of not recognising myself whenever I tried looking in the mirror. There was no one looking back at me. I was afraid and I thought I needed a guide to wake me up and bring me back to life.

There was this elderly African-Caribbean woman who intrigued me. She was frightened of evil occurrences and things she could not see. She'd regressed into becoming a frightened child. To protect herself, she had drawn crosses all over her body with cigarette ash. One day while sitting down for dinner, I said to her 'Are you Rosa Parks?'

'You could say that we are of the same spirit,' she said.

'How did you get here?'

'You could say that Rosa and I are sisters. Both of us very upset with how our children have been mistreated and killed. I suppose it is my fate to be here. The Devil is trying to possess me but my faith in Jesus is strong.'

I don't know why I expected the woman who sparked the civil rights movement in America to be in a mental hospital. There was something dignified about the demeanour of the woman I spoke to. Her shoes were tattered and worn out as if she had walked hundreds of miles in them. I could hardly make out the words she said because of the clatter in the dining room but there was a kindness in her voice and eyes. I wanted to be close for her to tell me about the things she had experienced and teach me how to overcome the dragon of death.

Shimon, a heavy Orthodox Jewish man, came over to me and kissed me on the cheek. 'I love you,' he said. He often got distressed and walked up and down the corridor agitatedly calling for his mother. 'Imma, Imma,' he would bellow. When he calmed down, I used to watch him praying with his Torah in his hand at the ashtray mounted on the wall. It was surreal to see this gentle loving man, beseeching Yahweh in front of the smoke of cigarettes that had not been stubbed out and worked as incense for his prayers.

Before long, I understood that we were all forsaken. Soon, I realised again that I could be whoever, whatever I wanted to be. I was a mental patient. I had been in this state so many times that I was now an expert. One day, sitting in the "Quiet Room", I began singing. Nobody cared or blinked. It was normal. My tremulous voice rose up...

> Trouble in mind
> I'm blue, but I won't be blue always
> Sun's gonna shine in my back door someday
> I'm gonna lay my head on some lonesome railroad line
> 2.19 come train ease my troubled mind.

*

When the time came to return home to my new family, some of the patients came to say goodbye to me. In such a nice way, they showed their concern and friendship, by reminding me that I was now a man with responsibilities towards my wife and baby and that I should keep taking my prescribed medicines.

9

Not long ago, while playing in the kitchen, Hayal looked up and asked me with shining eyes. 'Michael, you miss your mummy?'

'Yes, I do.' I replied.

'Don't worry. She's with angels. I'm here.' Then she paused. 'Do you love your mummy very much?'

'I do.'

'Don't worry, you can love me now.'

I called my mother every day. It was essentially to soothe her worries about me and to reassure myself that she loved me. The umbilical cord joining us remained intact until the end of her life. She had held me close to her womb and we were never really able to let go of each other. I still wanted to be received by her and be born her child in the eternal cycle of reincarnation. Often, I see my mother reflected in Hayal's gestures and laughter, in the way she plays and eats her food.

Every thought and emotion was ingrained on the parchment-like skin of my mother's face. She had an awesome presence. I'm looking at her photographs now: there is honesty, immense pride, strength touched with vulnerability, and a beauty that is more Native American than Indian. When she heard about Hayal's birth, she praised God. She was happy and yet there was tiredness in her voice. She told me there were many things she wanted to do. She would carry and cradle Hayal, raise her and cook for Sevim and me.

She was old now, and she knew she wouldn't make it. 'When are you going to come and take me with you?' If only I had been able to lie to her and give her grounds for hope, then maybe she would have lived longer.

The last time the three of us met my mother was in the summer of 2008. Sevim and I had laid a new carpet in her bedroom where she spent most of her days, remembering her life and creating fantasies about the people around her. 'I know,' she would say. 'You are all asking when the old woman will die. But it seems to me that I will live for a long time. I'm not ready for it. My time hasn't come.'

We sat in the garden beneath the shade of her favourite plum tree and listened to her hum and sing old folk songs in her gravelly voice. For the last few years, she had been hobbling along with a cane and her shoulders had become a little stooped. She used to wake up around 7am, make her bed, and say her prayers. At 10am, she would go to the bathroom, gargle, brush her toothless mouth. I remember her sitting on the edge of her bed or on her high chair, combing her fine grey hair, listening to Panjab Radio.

She had a new story to tell every day, despite never leaving her room. The last time I saw her, two days before I lost her, she didn't say much. The narratives were either too awful to be told or had come to a natural end without any conclusion. We sat silently in the twilight listening to old songs on the radio. Outside, there was a light flurry of snowflakes and the evening was becoming quieter. My mother was reading me with her intense gaze and smiled. 'Long hair suits you. You should wear a turban. You look so much like your daddy.'

She remembered the common in London where we used to walk when she visited Sevim and me. Because of the way she looked directly at people and let loose her infectious smile, they would come and talk to us as we sat on a bench. She thought people were either beautiful or ugly from the softness of the language they used. Once, an attractive African-Caribbean woman stopped and said, 'You look so young. What a lovely smile you have.' My mother, who understood very little of what she said, smiled even more. After she left, my mother turned to me and said, 'What a fine-looking woman. Aubergine is such a beautiful colour. Who can say we are not all God's people?'

Even though I always prolonged my stay with my mother, she sensed for the first time that I wanted to leave early. Despite both being in front of each other, it seemed we were present only in our own worlds, languishing inside memories of how each of us was yesterday. My name was always on her lips and she held my image in her eyes day and night. She was my place of heaven. I had grown up – to me, it felt like I had betrayed her. That night, she went hypoglycaemic. The ambulance paramedics gave her insulin and said she was safe. I decided to return to London, to my family. She knew I wanted to flee her. She was never angry with me. Mostly, she showed a magnanimous resignation that the object of her lifelong outpouring of love would someday have fallen from his pedestal.

Two days later, on a Thursday morning in 2009, she passed away. My middle brother, Atma, phoned me on my way to Broadcasting House for a meeting with BBC commissioning editors to see if I could get any work. I got off the 73 bus at Angel and stepped into the freezing downpour. I was weeping. 'My poor mummy,' I cried. I walked all the way back home to Stoke Newington. The house was empty. Sevim and Hayal were at a parent-and-toddler group. I could feel my mother's spirit communing with me, and I wanted so much to hold her and tell her not to be afraid. Instead, it was her voice that I heard comforting me, saying, 'Don't cry, Michael. All is well. Dying doesn't scare me.'

The funeral took place a week later. The hearse bearing her in a cheap wooden coffin pulled up. The rain had abated. A golden sun broke through the clouds. It was February, but all four seasons seemed to have come at once: winter, spring, summer, and autumn were manifest in the few days after she had died. We were waiting around in different rooms of my brother's comfortable Edwardian house. Seeing the coffin in the front yard prompted some of us to begin intoning, 'Waheguru, Waheguru.' Wonderful Lord, who guides us from darkness to light. The words seemed hollow. For me, the god of religion had died and I fostered an argumentative relationship with the divine inside.

Angie, my sister's daughter, began sobbing in the kitchen and her cousins went to comfort her. Hayal ran to the commotion and gently moved through the throng. Angie sat with her head in her arms. There, at her knee, Hayal reached up and touched her. She was comforting Angie but it was also like she was blessing her. Angie looked up tearfully and began laughing.

Hayal had been looking for her grandmother around the house. She became anxious when she only found the walking cane but not the owner. I guessed she would miss her.

10

It has been raining and the drip, drip, drip of water falling from the leaking gutter onto the debris in the garden can still be heard. There is the sound of the trains shunting towards White Hart Lane, occasionally blowing their horns. Police sirens travelling across a cold December night. My attention is attuned to the baby monitor, looking out for signs of Hayal stirring from her sleep. We're alone in the house. Sevim has taken some much-needed precious time to go meet some friends. I'm searching for words to write, but all I feel is the anxiety of looking after Hayal by myself.

Murat popped around earlier today as usual to see her. They played together in the basement. He likes pretending to be a dog chasing after her, while she runs laughing and shouting as if she is scared. He finds it difficult to say goodbye. He hovers around the door while about to leave.

'I love you,' he says.

'I love you too,' Hayal replies.

*

Christmas is approaching. Hayal is counting down the days when Santa Claus and the angels will come visit us. Last Sunday, we attended the Advent celebration at St. Paul's Steiner School set in an imposing Victorian church that, for many years, had stood abandoned and dilapidated. Evergreen winter branches and leaves, laid in the shape of a spiral symbolising the movement of the cosmos, adorned the stone-clad floor of the nave. A solo violin played welcoming us into the atmospheric darkness. The three of us sat next to each other, happy and contented listening to the lonely melancholic music. I felt grateful to Sevim for her constancy. My illnesses had tired her over the years. Now she was in possession of an unerring happiness. We smiled at each other, acknowledging the mysterious bond that connected us. I felt humbled by Sevim's generous spirit that had cleansed me of my shame of being mentally ill. Sometimes, I felt safe enough to lower my defences and forgive myself for the hardship I had inadvertently caused her. Hayal couldn't stop wriggling, her eyes radiating brightly her love for us and life.

Every child made the journey with a parent, following the spiral, carrying an unlit wax candle stuck in a red apple, towards a single source of fire and light that burnt in the centre.

I watched Sevim and Hayal emotionally when it came to their turn. They walked hand-in-hand. Hayal preciously clutched her candle. Every little step taken in the gloaming half-light was special. The darkness in the nave began dissolving as each child, in their eternal innocence, took the light and symbolically brought it back to illuminate the world. I understood, looking at my wife and daughter, that my time had come to reconcile with the Creative Light that I had tried to admonish and perhaps even put out.

11

I went to see Peter to ask if I could come off the medication.

I was the first to arrive at Harley Street. I was early. The Norwegian spruce Christmas tree glistened with twinkly red-and-yellow lights in the empty waiting room. I sat rehearsing what I would say to Peter. It had been a long time, partly because I couldn't afford to see him, but mostly because I was afraid of what he might say. I heard his voice as he entered and my heart skipped. He greeted me as usual, holding out his hand, smiling broadly like Gabriel Oak in *Far from the Madding Crowd*. I followed him up the galleried stairwell into his rooms on the first floor. I always remember sitting there for the first time, doused in bright summer sunlight which made me squint, while he and Sevim sat in the cool shade.

Peter's therapy sessions are a little like poetry. He unearths the seed hidden inside each session, the flower of which is a broken self. Over fifty minutes, a patient undergoes a benign ordeal of facing a symbolic death. The emotional turbulence present in one's being is distilled, leaving only the residue of what is meaningful in one's life. Peter has become the gatekeeper helping me unlock the secrets of my heart.

'How are you?' Peter asked.

'I'm well,' I replied. Then I explained my reason for seeing him.

'I'm glad that you've decided to come off the lamotrigine. I agree, three years is a long time. I don't believe existential problems can be medicated away indefinitely. Besides, the antipsychotic will be your backup.' He paused and put his hands together. 'And how are things with your wife and child?'

The unresolved issues associated with my becoming psychotic at Hayal's birth and my feeling that I had abandoned her and Sevim ached in my chest. It was a theme Peter and I had addressed before. He was familiar with complaints that I levelled against Sevim.

'Things are better now between Sevim and me,' I said. 'Ever since we've been having couple counselling, we've matured in our understanding of each other and our needs. As for Hayal, we're bonding together much better. She's a very precocious child. She can already speak Turkish and English fluently and understands Punjabi.'

My pause prompted him. 'And do you have any worries regarding her?'

Everything that had gone before had been pleasant but a little technical. Our conversation now became meaningful. It took its own direction, as I began telling him my concerns when it came to my daughter.

'I don't know what I can pass onto Hayal. I read this article in the *Guardian* about people in government, who were educated at public schools and Oxbridge. They have this great sense of entitlement. They know they belong here, and believe it is their right to be the ruling elite.'

'But Michael, you are as British as I am and belong here.'

'No, I don't feel that way. I was born of immigrant parents who had no education. My father used to cry when he went to India, leaving us behind. And he would cry when he returned. After a while we forgot where we belonged. Like him, I am in limbo.'

'And who is there in India for you?'

'There is no one left – everyone in the village has either left or died. My father and mother's history is vanishing. They have become part of a missing generation, and I feel myself being propelled towards the same fate. I don't know what I can offer my daughter in the way of belonging. I might be British and I'm grateful for being here, but my soul is Indian. Hayal is the embodiment of several cultures and I wonder what legacy she will carry from me, and the place she will have in this society.'

Peter looked at me thoughtfully. He spoke choosing his words carefully.

'It's impossible to say what will be passed down to succeeding generations. But I can say that one can live for the sixty or seventy years duration that a natural life-span allows. Or one can, if one wishes, live to be one hundred or six hundred years. It all depends on your vision for saving the missing generations and what you would like the future to become.'

EPILOGUE

Micah:

With what shall I come before the Lord
And bow myself before God on high?
Shall I give my first-born for my transgression,
The fruit of my body for the sin of my soul?'
He has showed you, O man, what is good;
And what does the Lord require of you
But to do justice, and to love kindness,
And to walk humbly with your God?

*

As I walked out of Peter's office, down the Euston Road, past the immaculate Georgian mansions of Regent's Park, I felt a sense of fearless elation. The heaviness in my head and heart had eased. I put on my headphones and began listening to the final stanzas of the Ninth Master, Guru Tegh Bahadur's psalm, Salok Mahalla 9:

Nothing is stable or permanent
Whatever has been created shall be destroyed
Everyone shall perish today or tomorrow
Nanak sing the glorious praises of the Lord
And give up the web of all entanglements

A picture of all my dead friends, relatives and forgotten generations played across the tableau of my mind. The wind blew through my hair. I crossed the road and continued walking determinedly. I didn't want to shake aside the mental images of the dead that no longer disturbed me, but rather made me feel connected and whole.

Not so long ago Hayal, deep in thought, asked me: 'Why do people die?'

'I don't know. Why do you think?' I said, feeling a little awkward.

'Well it's because if no one died the world would get to be very crowded.'

I saw my father sitting, feasting, together with all his friends and sages, at a long table in the foothills of the Himalayas. They exist in my mind and soul and of all those who know them. There are fertile lands and dimensions, which we can scarcely imagine, buried deep within us, from where those we love and hate come and go. I am thankful for the tears that I have found so difficult to cry, but now they stream and are like baptisms for my heart. They flow delicately like pearls falling into an ocean that one must cross to go forever beyond the limitations of this present life.

The vistas of my imagination fluttered like a Buddhist prayer flag. It seemed to me that blossom was pouring out of the mouth of the goldfishes swimming in their tank in our kitchen. Snow glittered on the mountains that tumbled down to kiss the freezing Indus River. Slender trees bent and moaned to the river's roar. I looked above into the dull grey London sky. My eyes were pools catching the pale light flooding down through the sunless chilled atmosphere. The steady stream of cars had come to halt in a traffic jam on the Euston Road. My attention was elsewhere – turned inwards to my mind, where at last I saw not only the desolation of death but also felt the poignant truth of resurrection itself.

*

The digital clock on the boiler is ticking away. Hayal is sleeping peacefully after a long day. I hear Sevim, busily tapping away on the computer in the bedroom, while I sit anticipating getting off my chair having completed this work. It's past midnight and soon I will go to bed having kissed Hayal goodnight. I am feeling the cold. I sense that my seeking is over. All is well – I am made resplendent with joy. The fire of death and the birth of love have cleansed me. My anger and imperfections are naïve once more. My struggle is over. I'm inspired to feel the caress of life again lighter than a feather, and it is as if my own mother and father are comforting me after what seemed an eternity.

ACKNOWLEDGEMENTS

I am deeply indebted to the individuals who, over many years, made it possible for this book to reach completion and see the light of day.

Many thanks to Dr Robin Lawrence and Dr Sander Kooij who saw me at different periods of breakdown and tempered my scepticism of psychiatry with their compassion and honesty.

I am grateful to several therapists who walked with me on my journey. Kay Lawrence was there. Special mention goes to Heidi Cohen, whose unfaltering belief in this work and kindness picked me up and helped me write to the end.

Among the many beautiful friends, I have to thank Peter Simpson, for the long insightful conversations; Yifat Fellner-Simpson, Talya Ezrahi, Frank Carr, Zeynep Putkeli for their generous time and care; and, of course, Khalid Khan who I really must make time to visit.

Claudia Zylbersztajn who gave me a job knowing my history, thank you. Mark Thomas Kelly for his presence and Leticia Costain for your wisdom. Some friends I made in mental hospitals: Ahmet, Shimon, and the inimitable David.

I must thank my family who supported me all these years with great patience. Nabkiran Angie Kaur Jhagra with whom I am able to talk freely; Rikki Jhagra and Murat Metin who encouraged me; Gulsum Metin, Sheriban Metin, and Leyla who grounded me; and Geoff Marshall.

I wish to thank my publishers at Trigger for bringing me in from the cold. Without your belief there would be no book. Special thanks go to my editor, Kasim Mohammed, for his trust and diligence.

REFERENCES

1 **Shakespeare, William.** (1604). 'Othello'. Retrieved from https://www.owleyes.org/text/othello [accessed 15.07.19]

2 **Dosti.** (1964). Dir. Satyen Bose. [accessed 15.07.19]

3 **Raat Aur Din.** (1967). Dir. Satyen Bose. [accessed 15.07.19]

4 **Heraclitus.** (500 BCE). Retrieved from https://www.ancient.eu/article/182/heraclitus-fragments/ [accessed 15.07.19]

5 **Leadbelly.** (1940). 'Ain't Gonna Study War No More'. Retrieved from https://youtu.be/pNkrsejvnCc [accessed 15.07.19]

TRIGGER™

The mental health & wellbeing publisher

www.triggerpublishing.com

Trigger is a publishing house devoted to opening conversations about mental health. We tell the stories of people who have suffered from mental illnesses and recovered, so that others may learn from them.

Adam Shaw is a worldwide mental health advocate and philanthropist. Now in recovery from mental health issues, he is committed to helping others suffering from debilitating mental health issues through the global charity he co-founded, The Shaw Mind Foundation. www.shawmindfoundation.org

Lauren Callaghan (CPsychol, PGDipClinPsych, PgCert, MA (hons), LLB (hons), BA), born and educated in New Zealand, is an innovative industry-leading psychologist based in London, United Kingdom. Lauren has worked with children and young people, and their families, in a number of clinical settings providing evidence based treatments for a range of illnesses, including anxiety and obsessional problems. She was a psychologist at the specialist national treatment centres for severe obsessional problems in the UK and is renowned as an expert in the field of mental health, recognised for diagnosing and successfully treating OCD and anxiety related illnesses in particular. In addition to appearing as a treating clinician in the critically acclaimed and BAFTA award-winning documentary *Bedlam*, Lauren is a frequent guest speaker on mental health conditions in the media and at academic conferences. Lauren also acts as a guest lecturer and honorary researcher at the Institute of Psychiatry Kings College, UCL.